Called to Participate

Theological, Ritual, and Social Perspectives

Mark Searle

Barbara Searle
and
Anne Y. Koester,
Editors

LITURGICAL PRESS
Collegeville, Minnesota

www.litpress.org

Cover design by Joachim Rhoades, O.S.B.

1	2	3	4	5	6	7	8

Library of Congress Cataloging-in-Publication Data

Searle, Mark, 1941–
   Called to participate : theological, ritual, and social perspectives / [author], Mark Searle ; Barbara Searle, and Anne Y. Koester, editors.
      p. cm.
   Summary: "A theology of liturgical prayer and participation"—Provided by publisher.
   Includes bibliographical references and index.
   ISBN-10: 0-8146-2942-3 (pbk. : alk. paper)
   ISBN-13: 978-0-8146-2942-0 (pbk. : alk. paper)
   1. Public worship—Catholic Church. 2. Catholic Church—Liturgy—Theology. 3. Liturgical movement—Catholic Church. I. Searle, Barbara Schmich. II. Koester, Anne Y. III. Title.

BX1970.15.S43 2005
264'.02--dc22   2005005116

Dedication

"We can justly consider that
the future of humanity
lies in the hands of those
who are strong enough
to provide coming generations
with reasons for living and hoping"
(*Gaudium et Spes*, 31).

To

Anna Clare
Matthew Thomas
and
Justin Francis

Your father's legacy of faith
for you
and for your generation.

Contents

Foreword

ESSENTIALS FOR UNDERSTANDING THIS BOOK

Mark Searle was working on this manuscript during his illness and approaching death († 1992). Although his creative process usually consisted of extensive reading, copious note taking, and a long period of preoccupation and incubation, culminating in the production of a nearly perfect first draft, this manuscript was different. The illness had affected his cognitive processing, and his writing was marked by free association; he included ideas and quotations of seemingly everything that had been important in his approach to liturgy. The final text sounded like parts of St. John's Gospel—passionate but repetitive. Even though I had promised him on his deathbed that I would see to getting this manuscript published, I entertained the thought of breaking that promise when I finally began the editing process. There was surely a book there, but it was a book within a book, and nearly half became like the marble Michaelangelo chipped away to reveal an underlying form. What emerged in the end was something of Mark Searle's last will and testament for the praying Church. *Called to Participate* is what he would have wanted us to know and live.

For some time he had been concerned about the state of liturgical renewal and was trying to pull together the perspectives he had been developing through his teaching, writing, and international lecturing. He chose to organize them around the topic of liturgical participation because for him it was an essential if sometimes misunderstood aspect of the renewal. In his 1988 *Commonweal* article, "Renewing the Liturgy—Again," he wrote, "In general, liturgical practice reveals a widespread failure to grasp the *theological* import of the concept of participation. In part, this may be the result of the very process of introducing changes which, despite the catechetical effort led by Paul VI himself, tended to focus popular attention on the practical aspects of liturgical change rather than on the mystery at the heart of the liturgical event. The profound spiritual meaning of liturgical participation was overshadowed by the problem of how to get everybody to join in the singing."[1]

Mark Searle's English birth and foreign education enabled him to be ever the keen observer of North American life and ecclesiastical agendas. As a student of history and culture, the contexts for liturgy, he understood that the post-Vatican II renewal was situated in a particular moment of time. He often wrote about modernity and how it shaped the issues before and after the council. Drawing on the work of historians, social scientists, and ritual scholars,[2] he saw modernity's chief characteristics to be a breaking from established tradition and authority, a resultant pluralism and belief in the myth of progress, and an eventual massification[3] of society and loss of communal values. In order for people to deal with these rapid and novel developments in the history of the world, emphasis was shifted to the individual life. The individualism of our time, he wrote, "is less a moral fault than it is a cultural mindset that has developed by trying to make necessity into a virtue and turn the loss of community into a gain for the individual person."[4]

He saw that the practice of religion, not immune to the effects of modernity, has undergone a move toward privatization that leaves the individual the sole arbiter of ultimate values and undermines the bonds that can create genuine community. "What holds us together now as a people, as a nation," he said, "is not, as in the past, a common world view, a sacred cosmos, a shared conviction about what constitutes a well-lived life, but our mutual dependency on patterns of production and consumption into which we are socialized by secular education and the mass media." But even in the midst of this experience of life, our need for community is not destroyed. Rather we have attempted to satisfy it with manageable forms, putting high priority on close and intimate relationships, groups who share common interests, and serial commitments. In a highly complex and mobile society, those possibilities seem the best we can envision. "The cult of intimacy, like radical individualism," he wrote, "is less an ethical failure or a social ill in and of itself than it is an unreflective cultural response to the conditions of modernity. It is not an expression of ultimate selfishness, but a blind response to a threat to cultural survival."

As cognizant as he was of the spirit of the times, Mark Searle was more thoroughly imbued with the spirit of the Second Vatican Council. He came into liturgical leadership just as the council was closing, and he never failed to promulgate the messages not only of the Constitution on the Sacred Liturgy but key documents that undergirded the experience of the liturgy, especially the documents on Revelation and Church. Like other leaders, he hoped the liturgical changes would contribute to the vitality of the Church and the larger world. But in his last years he was beginning to wonder if the liturgical reforms, while necessary, were perhaps not sufficient. "We have reformed the rites according to conciliar directives and our own best notions of what they were supposed to look like, but our ideas of what they were supposed to look like have perhaps been colored more by our secular culture than the tradition they were meant to vivify." He saw that culture was impacting the reformed liturgy in ways never imagined even by those who advocated acculturation. In a hundred minute ways, he observed, the liturgy celebrated in any given church on any given day is profoundly marked by the cultural context, a context that is largely invisible to the participants because they live within it. That the individual is set over against the community; that society itself is seen as a conglomeration of individuals rather than the individual's being the product of the culture; that one's individual judgments are preferred over the judgment of tradition or authority; that the quest for self-realization is placed ahead of the pursuit of the common good; that responsibility for public affairs is relinquished to bureaucrats and technocrats; that personal freedom is given priority over social responsibility—these realities are in the air we breathe; they affect the way we have reformed our liturgies and how we pray them. Despite their differences in style, he noted, the lively family celebration on Sunday morning and the final weekend Eucharist on Sunday night, the highly emotive liturgy and the impersonal routinized liturgy, equally reflect modernity and/or the reactions against it.

He recognized that different people, depending on their own liturgical experiences and their own implicit or explicit criteria, would generalize differently about the state of liturgy, but he thought all would share a common investment in the question, "Where do we go from here?" He himself did not wish to decry modernism or minimize the gains of the last two hundred years in terms of respect for the inviolable dignity of the human person, the elaboration and safeguarding of human freedoms or the improvement in living standards. Nor did he think pluralism would merely "go away." He thought rather that we ought to explore the implications of what it means to be Church within a pluralistic society and what it means to be baptized into such a Church. He thought that the responses we have come up with so far in learning to live with pluralism—radical individualism and pseudo-community—simply would not suffice. "Far from endorsing these features of our time," he wrote, "the Church should be resisting them and cooperating with those who are developing alternatives."

Mark Searle's speaking, writing, and teaching offered his audiences alternatives about entering into the liturgy. Using his facility with ritual studies and the social sciences, as well as his theological and spiritual depths, he always tried to envision new ways of relating the individual to the Church and the Church to the larger world. This work is no exception. Although he did not have the luxury of working it out in as much detail as some of his other writings, the lines of his alternative and synthetic vision are present. The reader, however, will find nothing here that can be implemented per se. Instead, what can be found is an invitation to all people in the Church to participate in liturgy according to its very nature and, in so doing, to realize an essential aspect of their Christian vocation.

Chapter 1 presents an historical perspective, delineating not one but two liturgical movements, that offers complementary approaches to the task of renewing the liturgy. Each has its own way of conceptualizing participation in the liturgy. The earlier movement "brought people to the liturgy," while the more recent one "brought liturgy to the people." By searching out the roots of the early liturgical movement, he lays out an alternative emphasis that can enrich our own post-Vatican II efforts at continued renewal and more engagement in liturgical prayer.

Chapter 2 invites people into the liturgy by describing the nature of the complex event: liturgy as ritual activity, liturgy as the work of Christ, and liturgy as sharing in the life of God. He sees these as three successively deeper levels of participation, each with its own discipline and its own language, moving from the visible to the invisible, from the human to the divine. Taken together they constitute what he calls the *inward* or *contemplative* dimension of liturgy.

Chapter 3 looks at selected aspects of the liturgy, the proclamation of the Word, the prayers of the liturgy, its gestures, and finally the very time that surrounds it. He addresses each aspect from a contemplative perspective, showing how a participant might move from the ritual level into the action of Christ and on to the sharing of the divine life of the Trinity. He describes what it would mean in each instance to submit to ritual constraints, to take on the work of Christ and ultimately to experience heaven on earth.

The final chapter looks at the complementary dimension of the liturgy, its *outward* or *public* aspect. He explores the inherently social character of the liturgy, which points beyond any particular gathered assembly and draws its participants into a unity that transcends space and time. To respond to this invitation is to participate in God's work in human history with all the social and political consequences that entails.

Called to Participate will require some stretching from most of us in order to assimilate all three levels of liturgical participation as well as liturgy's inner and outer dimensions. Mark Searle noted more than once that the liturgical movement was, at its best, also an ascetical movement, calling us to return to the sources of the common spiritual life and to take up the discipline inherent in the Christian vocation.

Those reading this book more than a decade after it was written will find some emphases less pertinent than they once were and some current issues unaddressed, but the basic message to be one that is both timeless and timely. He alludes to the full sweep of salvation history and invites us to take our place in it. He acknowledges that this will demand nothing short of a revolution as we shift our focus from individual concerns to common causes, from a small worldview to a catholic worldview, in the largest sense of that word. It was Mark Searle's genuine desire to contribute to a contemporary spirituality that was firmly rooted in the liturgy and to continue the ongoing work of liturgical renewal which must be accomplished in every generation.

On a final note, I want to express my heartfelt gratitude to several people who over the years have contributed in various ways to the process of readying this book for publication—whether locating sources Mark Searle cited, reading and commenting on the text, or doing the tedious task of copy editing the manuscript: Martin Connell, Nathan Mitchell, J. Frank Henderson, Virginia Sloyan, and Mary Jo Huck. This book would not have come to be without the attention to detail and liturgical expertise of the co-editor, Anne Koester, and so I publicly acknowledge my debt of gratitude to her. Finally, I also want to thank Mark Twomey of Liturgical Press for his enthusiasm for publishing the book and his patience in awaiting the final product.

Barbara Searle

Notes

1. "Renewing the Liturgy—Again," *Commonweal* (November 18, 1988) 620.

2. Some of the writers cited in earlier versions of this material are Edward Shils, Peter Berger, David Martin, Martin Marty, George Lindbeck, Ronald Grimes, and Francis Mannion. Every effort has been made to credit authors whose ideas influenced and were incorporated by Mark Searle, but a posthumous work has certain inevitable limits. Future editions of this work will correct any errors brought to our attention.

3. Mark Searle described "massification" as a "stage in the evolution of a society where the different social institutions have become so specialized and the ordering of society so complex that the democratic process can no longer work effectively. Instead, basic decisions affecting the life of the people are made by technocrats, and most of the population, losing perspective and control, are 'maneuvered by the mass media to the point where they believe nothing they have not heard on the radio, seen on television, or read in the newspapers.' As the fate of our lives rests in the hands of fewer and fewer people further and further away, we are rendered powerless in our own society, incapable of engaging effectively in the direction of its processes." "Private Religion, Individualistic Society, and Common Worship," *Vision: The Scholarly Contributions of Mark Seale to Liturgical Renewal*, eds. Anne Y. Koester and Barbara Searle (Collegeville: Liturgical Press, 2004) 188, quoting, Paulo Freire, *Education for Critical Consciousness* (New York: Continuum, 1973) 34.

4. This and uncited quotations that follow are Mark Searle's and have been taken from drafts of chapters not included in this final edition.

1   Two Liturgical Movements; Two Approaches to Participation

Historians usually see the liturgical movement that led to the reforms of Vatican II as unfolding in several phases: first, the monastic phase, associated with Solesmes and Beuron and Maria Laach; second, the pastoral phase, associated with Lambert Beauduin, Pius Parsch, Virgil Michel, and others between the wars; and finally, the reform phases culminating in the liturgy constitution of the Second Vatican Council. Such periodicization of history, of course, is always somewhat artificial. This particular way of reading the modern history of the liturgy approaches it from the point of view of the leaders and centers of innovation: the Benedictine restoration of the nineteenth century, the pastoral radiation of liturgical consciousness from such centers as Mont César, Klosterneuberg, and Collegeville in the first half of the twentieth century, and the networking of advocates of liturgical reform in regional and international conferences after World War II.

If instead of focusing on places and personalities, however, the historian were to focus on agendas, the history of the liturgical movement would seem less evolutionary, more discontinuous. Indeed, one could then more accurately speak of two liturgical movements. The first was countercultural in inspiration, aimed at weaning nineteenth- and early twentieth-century Catholics from their culturally accommodated devotions and their individualistic piety and bringing them back to the liturgy. The second movement grew out of the first but worked in the opposite direction and with the conviction that the liturgy had to be accommodated to the people. The first movement was driven by the strong belief that liturgy could re-form Catholics as a People of God to be reckoned with socially and politically. The second recognized that for liturgy to have an impact on the people, it would have to be brought closer to them, for example, through the use of the vernacular. A more thorough look at these two movements is in order.

THE FIRST LITURGICAL MOVEMENT:
SOCIAL TRANSFORMATION THROUGH LITURGICAL FORMATION

What was most distinctive about the early liturgical movement, I think, was that its proponents saw it chiefly as a means for revivifying Catholic life and for preparing Catholics to take an active role in the re-shaping of contemporary society. The heightened appreciation of the liturgy that they preached and practiced was not an aesthetic appreciation so much as a practical and theological appreciation of its social potential. This did not mean that all saw the desired outcome in the same terms; as we shall see, this was largely a function of their particular historical and cultural experience. But they were all concerned about the need for Catholics to take on the social ills of their day. For this the faithful would need both a new vantage point from which to recognize those ills and a new source of energy from which to draw for the construction of an alternative social order. Unlikely as it must have seemed to most of their contemporaries, they saw the best chance for such a transformation to lie with the ancient, encrusted, largely ignored, and almost entirely fossilized public worship life of the Church.

Prosper Guéranger (1805–1875)

The origins of the movement in the Catholic Church that led to the liturgical reforms of Vatican II are often sought in the life and work of a French priest who in 1833 reopened an abandoned priory just outside the small town of Solesmes. Since then the priory has grown into an archabbey with a formidable reputation for musical scholarship, its name synonymous for many with Gregorian chant. But in 1833 it was a ruin, one of hundreds of religious establishments that had fallen victim to the political, social, and religious upheavals of the previous half century, that is, the French Revolution and the Napoleonic wars.

In continental Europe and especially in France, the 1789 revolution and its aftermath were far more of a watershed than the Reformation had ever been. The 1790 *Civil Constitution of the Clergy* had basically co-opted the Church as a branch of the state: its clergy and bishops were required to take an oath of loyalty to the government from which, henceforth, they would receive their appointments and their salaries. Since no value was attached in those secularized times to contemplative prayer, monastic communities were disbanded and religious life outlawed except for those who were active in such socially useful roles as teachers and nurses. Moreover, the whole system of ecclesiastical administration was rationalized. Dioceses were reorganized to match the boundaries of local government administration, with the result that a number of ancient sees were suppressed, and others, with quite different liturgical traditions (for many did not follow the post-Tridentine Roman rite), were simply amalgamated. Parish churches were kept open only where there was sufficient population to justify a salaried clergyman; many were simply closed down and the properties sold off.

The closure, confiscation, sale, and (often) demolition of churches and religious houses had an immediate visual impact on France and struck a tremendous blow to the Church's omnipresence and power there. But the takeover of ecclesiastical property was merely one symptom of a whole new mindset that had come to dominate this traditionally Catholic nation and that was in the ascendancy all over Europe and in the newly independent United States of America. The new masters of France were rationalists, believing in the possibility, if not the inevitability, of human progress and seeing in the Church and its teachings and practices a major force for obscurantism, ignorance, and superstition. Religious faith seemed to many the enemy of human reason. Religious practices seemed but a reactionary clinging to the very superstitions of the past that stood in the way of a new future for humanity.

Thus the industrial and political upheavals surrounding the turn of the century transformed the experience of life in Europe by profoundly altering the traditional social structures and the habits of mind that had sustained them. At the grassroots level, this meant an enormous amount of insecurity and suffering, of crime, violence, and immorality. The first half of the nineteenth century saw a number of concerned attempts to diagnose the damage done to the social fabric and to propose new forms of human community. Karl Marx was undoubtedly the most trenchant critic of the new industrial society, but he was only one of many would-be reformers at work in both the old and the new countries.

Prosper Guéranger belongs to this same movement, though his analyses of the situations and thus his responses to them were entirely different from those of Karl Marx. Guéranger was inclined to blame the collapse of the Church in France and the rise of the new free thinkers on the unresolved tensions in the French church of the eighteenth century, where the Jansenist controversy and its aftermath, coupled with the nationalistic tendencies of the episcopate, had created a gap between Rome and French Catholicism.

For Guéranger, the only true response to the questions of human existence was to be found in Christianity, but the only authentic Christianity was one that was free of the tyranny of intellectual fashions and able to stand above petty national interests as a truly universal religion. Thus Guéranger came to promote loyalty to Rome, rather than loyalty to the traditions of the French church or to its episcopate. But it was above all in the fixed liturgy of the Roman Church that he saw a pattern of life and action strong enough to be able to withstand the transient fashions of thought and culture. Only the liturgy of the Roman Church—as opposed to the conflicting traditions of the French dioceses and rationalizings of the "neo-Gallican" reforms of liturgical books—could knit the social fabric back together and give people a sense once more of being part of something larger than themselves. Liturgy, in Guéranger's view, was the real matrix of Christian identity because it was not the prayer and devotion of individual Christians but the prayer of the whole Church; it was not susceptible to the whims of individuals here and now but was the tradition inherited from the saints of all the ages. In the celebration of a fixed, objective, formal liturgy belonging to the whole Church, Guéranger saw the individual transcending his or her own self and the narrowness of his or her own life of private joys and sorrows to become part of God's work in history.

Pius X (1835–1914)

Some scholars see Guéranger's work as being no more than a prelude to the real liturgical movement which they would date from Pius X in the early twentieth century. It was Pius X, after all, who encouraged frequent Communion, restored plainchant to the churches, undertook a reform of the breviary, and encouraged the active participation of the faithful in the celebration of the liturgy. He even gave serious consideration to a general reform of the whole liturgy of the Latin Church. But Pius X was also the pope who condemned "Modernism" and set Catholic biblical and theological scholarship back by several decades. He was the pope who required that candidates for holy orders and for teaching positions take the anti-modernistic oath, and who tolerated, if he did not instigate, a series of investigations in the Church comparable to those of the McCarthy era in the United States in the 1950s. These two faces of Pius X—his encouragement of the liturgy and his heresy hunting—are only intelligible against the background of his life and time.

Pius X was ordained to the priesthood and began his priestly ministry just at the point where Italy was in violent transition from being a collection of independent states to becoming a modern nation. This was the era of the *Risorgimento*, as it was called, and its leaders were mostly free thinkers of a very anticlerical kind. What was for Italy a *risorgimento*, a new beginning, was for the Church a traumatic wrenching involving the loss of the papal states, those large tracts of Italy running from Rome almost to Venice that had been part of the patrimony of Peter since the eighth century. From being a major temporal ruler (and thus free, it was thought, from domination by any secular power), the pope became the "prisoner of the Vatican," a diminution that seemed to many believers and unbelievers alike to be the harbinger of the end of the papacy and thus of the Church itself. Moreover, the political and social eclipse of the Church's temporal power was accompanied by the threat of an intellectual and cultural eclipse as well. The rise of scientific thought and of historical-critical methods seemed to undermine the very bases of Christian faith and to entail the end of religious beliefs and practices. To most people a hundred years ago the new sciences and the old faith seemed implacably hostile to one another, and all the advantage in the conflict seemed to lie with the new ways of thinking.

Having experienced the way this filtered down to ordinary people as a general disparagement of the sacred and a scorn for religious faith and practice, Pius X was determined to use all the means at his disposal to fight the modern world for the soul of Europe. But when he looked at his resources in the Church, he saw the vast majority of Catholics subsisting on a diet of sentimental piety and engaging in devotions that were peripheral to the central mysteries of faith, full of cheap emotionalism set to saccharine music. Everywhere he went he heard church music modeled on popular dance tunes and operettas, and the liturgy of the Church turned into a backdrop for decadent musical and artistic performances. Well before he became pope, first as bishop of Mantua and then as patriarch of Venice, he had become convinced that this sort of religiosity would never enable the Church to withstand the grave spiritual and cultural crisis of the times. A Church whose membership lived on forms of piety that were themselves deeply imbued with the spirit and tastes of the age was ill-equipped to reassert its own identity in a secularized and secularizing world.

The strategy he devised was one of drawing the faithful back into the ambit of the Church by recalling them to the basics of the Christian life, namely, the reception of Communion at the liturgy rather than private devotions to the Sacred Heart, Mary, or the saints and congregational singing of plainchant, instead of the amateur operettas that were so fashionable in church music circles. In both instances, the goal was to engage the faithful in the liturgical life and actions of the Church as a whole, instead of abandoning them to pursue their own devotional choices on the basis of purely personal taste.

In other words, like Prosper Guéranger, Pius X saw in the liturgy a means to counter the cultural tide and to restore social cohesion by giving people a sense of being part of something larger than themselves. As he put it in a now famous text:

> We are filled with a burning desire to see the true Christian spirit flourish in every respect and be preserved by all the people. We are therefore of the opinion that before everything else it is necessary to provide for the sanctity and dignity of the temple, where the faithful assemble for no other purpose than that of acquiring this spirit from its primary and indispensable fount, that is, the active participation in the most sacred mysteries and in the public and solemn prayer of the Church.[1]

For Pius X, the "Christian spirit" was at all points at odds with the spirit of the times, and his vision of a restored Christian order was quite expressly a restoration of feudal Christendom. But once again, as with Prosper Guéranger, one need not embrace his political views or endorse his methods of pursuing them in order to recognize that, like Guéranger, Pius X saw the liturgy as the means for making Catholics into Christians and for turning individuals who assuaged private needs with individualistic devotions into a force to stem the secularist tide of history. The liturgical changes he introduced were simply an invitation to priests and people to celebrate the liturgy in such a way that being shaped by it into a new solidarity, they might effectively contribute to the reshaping of society.

Virgil Michel, O.S.B. (1890–1938)

Virgil Michel shared the same view of the formative potential of the liturgy, but his political outlook was rather different from that of his illustrious predecessors. As a young Minnesotan of German extraction, he had joined the largely German-speaking abbey of St. John's in Collegeville, Minnesota when Pius X was pope. Ordained in 1916, he was sent for further studies at The Catholic University of America in Washington, D.C., and then, a few years later, to Sant' Anselmo in Rome, where he was supposed to study metaphysics, philosophy, social ethics, and economic theory. It was in Rome that he first met Lambert Beauduin, the Belgian Benedictine who had succeeded in launching a grassroots liturgical movement to educate clergy and laypersons in the new vision of the Church as Body of Christ and of liturgy as the corporate prayer of the Church. Through Beauduin, Virgil Michel became familiar with the theological underpinnings of the liturgical movement and with the means being used to promote it in Europe.

For all his enthusiasm for the liturgy, however, Virgil Michel never lost sight of his social and economic interests. He traveled widely in Europe, observing the alienation of the working classes from the Church, the poverty and insecurity that were their lot, and the ravages of laissez-faire capitalism. He was by now familiar with Leo XIII's great encyclical *Rerum novarum* (1891) and with the efforts of reformist bishops to propagate the message of social justice, but he also became acutely aware of how much the European church tended to side with the rich and powerful, and to ignore the needs of the workers.

Back in the United States, he witnessed from afar the consolidation of the Soviet Union as a totalitarian state under Stalin and the rise of new totalitarian governments in Spain, Italy, and Germany. Closer to home, he witnessed the effects of *laissez-faire* capitalism in the United States, leading to the Wall Street collapse of 1929 and the Great Depression. In Europe, Pope Pius XI was warning of the dangers of communism and socialism but seemed far less discomforted by the rise of fascism. In the U.S., the great danger to modern society, according to Virgil Michel, was neither socialism nor fascism but unbridled individualism. It was the cult of free enterprise, understood as the right to do business free of all government regulations, which had created the general supposition that progress would best be achieved if people pursued their own individual self-interest without regard to society's traditional claims on the individual's sense of responsibility.

For Virgil Michel, more than for anyone else, liturgical renewal went hand in hand with what was called, in those days, "social reconstruction" or "social regeneration." In 1935, he coined his famous syllogism:

> Pius X tells us that the liturgy is the indispensable source of the authentic Christian spirit. Pius XI says that the true Christian spirit is indispensable for social regeneration.
>
> Hence the conclusion: The liturgy is the indispensable basis for Christian social regeneration.[2]

Virgil Michel saw the liturgy as a practice, a learning-by-doing of the great truths of the Christian faith. These truths, forgotten in the privatistic devotional Catholicism of the nineteenth century, included the social dimension of the human person, the corporate character of the Church, the organic nature of society, the recognition that the Christian life is lived as part of a larger whole and for the sake of others, not just for the sake of oneself. He did not concern himself much in the 1930s with possible changes in the liturgy, but he wanted the existing rite to be celebrated well, and he wanted the faithful to understand that it was an essentially communitarian act. Liturgy, he felt, well done and properly understood, would generate an awareness of the social dimension of Christianity that would carry over into everyday life, into the world of daily living, of business, and of politics. Thus he could say:

> If the first purpose of the liturgical movement is to lead the faithful into more intimate participation in the liturgy of the Church, then the further objective must also be that of getting the liturgical spirit to radiate forth from the altar of Christ into every aspect of the daily life of the Christian.[3]

This, then, was one liturgical movement. Its goal was to adapt the people to the liturgy so that, thus transformed themselves, Catholics would then be in a position to contribute more effectively to the transformation of society.

THE SECOND LITURGICAL MOVEMENT: CHURCH RENEWAL THROUGH LITURGICAL REFORM

It is a little more difficult to be specific about names and places when it comes to the second liturgical movement. Growing imperceptibly out of the first movement and eventually replacing it, the second movement differed from its parent in that it focused more on the reform of the liturgy. This is not meant to suggest that change was being sought for its own sake. True, many of the leaders were historians who were profoundly aware of the ways in which, with the passage of time, developments had overtaken the practice of the liturgy that were "less harmonious with the intimate nature of the liturgy," especially its communal character.[4] Nonetheless, their motivation was less the restoration of the liturgy to its pristine state than the renewal of church life, which such a restoration was thought likely to produce. The motivation was ultimately pastoral, therefore, but in contrast to Guéranger, Pius X, and Virgil Michel, whose sights were fixed on social regeneration, the reformers were perhaps less inclined to look beyond the immediate ecclesial impact that was hoped for from their proposed reforms.

The second liturgical movement is harder to trace, but it may have begun in Nazi Germany. Under Hitler, the Catholic Church found itself deprived of its press, its Catholic trade unions, its educational institutions, and its charitable organizations. Under the pretext of limiting the church to its own proper sphere of influence (the otherworldly), the Nazis effectively deprived the church in Germany of everything but the Eucharist, the sacraments, and its devotional life. Under these circumstances, the church discovered the value of the liturgy as a Catholic antidote to the Hitler youth rallies and to the mythology of the German *Geist* and the German *Volk*. Despite the misgivings of some, the German bishops approved the newly burgeoning liturgical movement as the primary form of apostolate to German youth. It was in this context that demands for reform of the rites began to surface: requests for use of the vernacular, the use of German hymns at Mass, and the restoration of the Easter Vigil to its proper role as a night vigil.

To this one should also add the wartime experience of considerable numbers of French and Belgian priests and seminarians who had been drafted into the armed forces, captured by the Germans, and imprisoned in POW camps where, despite Red Cross inspections, they were frequently deprived of their religious rights. As a result, the Mass had to be celebrated furtively in the corner of a barracks with none of the customary vestments and sacred vessels, under conditions reminiscent of the participants of the earliest days of Christianity. When the war was over many priests who had experienced what the Eucharist could mean when celebrated in a hostile environment by a close-knit group of believers returned to their parish churches. They yearned to be able to share with their parishioners the experience of celebrating the liturgy under very different conditions—conditions in which the essentials stood out because so much else had been taken away.

Thus it came to pass that in the immediate postwar period, the movement for liturgical reform began to grow. Despite the fact that the ogre of National Socialism had yielded to the specter of international communism, the liturgical movement was becoming more concerned with liturgical renovation than with the construction of a new social order. From 1948 a secret commission appointed by Pius XII was at work preparing a general reform of the Roman liturgy, the fruits of whose work were the restoration of the Easter Vigil (1951) and a renewed order for the Holy Week liturgy (1955).

But while the general reform was being planned, Pius XII was already taking steps toward accommodating the liturgy to the people by giving permission to use the vernacular at marriages and funerals, the reduction of the eucharistic fast to three hours, and introducing evening Masses. And while all this was happening in Rome, the ground was being prepared in the rest of the Church. Popular missals were becoming increasingly common, the dialog Mass was introduced, talks and books on the liturgy were beginning to circulate. The National (later North American) Liturgical Weeks (1940–1975) brought together parishioners and scholars whose goal was the same as Pius XII, that is, to restore all things in Christ, which they believed would happen primarily in the Church's liturgy. At some point in this period the idea began to gain currency that increased participation in the liturgy required changes in the liturgy itself. By this was meant, above all, the introduction of the vernacular, at least in the readings at Mass. Then to the surprise of many in the Church, John XXIII called the council.

The Constitution on the Sacred Liturgy, debated and adopted early in the council's work, was a reforming document. It mandated a general reform of the Catholic liturgy, mainly on the grounds that its very nature requires the full, conscious, and active participation of all the faithful:

> Mother Church earnestly desires that all the faithful be led to that full, conscious and active participation in liturgical celebrations which is demanded by the very nature of the liturgy. Such participation by the Christian people . . . is their right and duty by reason of their baptism.
>
> In the restoration and promotion of the sacred liturgy, this full, conscious and active participation by all the people is the aim to be considered before else, for it is the primary and indispensable source from which the faithful are to derive the true Christian spirit.[5]

The opening paragraph of the liturgy constitution suggests that to vote for liturgical reform was to take a practical step toward realizing the overall purpose of Vatican II, namely, the deepening and broadening of the Christian sense of collective identity and mission. To this end, the council made it clear that it was set on changing not only the way Catholics performed the liturgy but the way we thought about it and thus the way we thought about ourselves as Church. If the new liturgy could not presuppose a conversion of mind and heart, it was hoped it might provoke one by calling Catholic Christians back to the basics of their common life in Christ.

The liturgy constitution is responsible for the remarkable transformation of the Church's worship life that we have witnessed in the past decades. There are few, surely, who would not rejoice at the resulting exposure of Catholic Christians to the Scriptures on a scale hitherto unknown. Some have criticized aspects of the new Lectionary, but the provision of such a vastly expanded repertoire of biblical readings and the decision to have them proclaimed in the vernacular have had a major and irreversible impact on Catholic life. Similarly, the retrieval of the liturgical year from its previous domination by feasts of saints, minor and major, mythical or real, has redirected attention, especially on Sundays, to sustained reflection on the central religious truths. So also with the return of the prayer of the People of God to their own languages, restoring a genuine process of Christian initiation for adults culminating in the Easter sacraments, successfully encouraging more frequent Communion, making available both bread and wine at Communion, actively engaging the assembly in the rites, and developing other ministries and functions along that of the presider—all of which are achievements of major significance in the life of the Church.

These and other changes fulfilled the expectation that the reformed rites were to be "within the people's powers of comprehension, and normally should not require much explanation."[6] That the rites would speak for themselves is perhaps the epitome of the movement to bring the liturgy to the people.

It was not ruled out that the people should adapt themselves to the liturgy or that they should be changed by their experience of the liturgy. Indeed, the liturgy constitution opens with a statement of the council's goals, which include the intensification of the daily growth of Catholics in Christian living. Nor was it ruled out that the liturgy should contribute to the work of the Church in the world, but unfortunately the relationship was not spelled out. As many have noted, while both the constitutions on the Church and on Divine Revelation contributed mightily to developing the theology of the Church and of the sacramental economy, the document on the Church in the world failed even to mention the Church's sacramental and liturgical life. This omission meant that a sense of the intrinsic link between liturgy and social action was largely lost in the immediate postconciliar period.

Thus we have had two liturgical movements, both of which have made important contributions to the life of the Church much as multiple movements enrich and deepen a symphony. The first focused on liturgical formation and social transformation, bringing people to the liturgy so that they might be empowered to go out and change the social order. The second focused on liturgical change and ecclesial renewal, bringing the liturgy to the people so that they might participate fully and help bring the Church into the modern world.

CONCLUSION: TOWARD A NEW SYNTHESIS

Today we have enough perspective on the postconciliar period to see the direction in which we have been going and enough perspective on the century leading up to the council to be able to compare our approach to liturgical reform with theirs. Looking back to the nineteenth- and early twentieth-century reformers might help us to see our own approaches more clearly and to frame the question, what shall we leave for those who come after us?

The vision of the first liturgical movement, that of liturgy creating a new sense of Church, of the liturgy as the place where the many discover their individual lives to be inextricably part of the one collective life in the Spirit, where the faithful are prepared for their work of social transformation has tended to be lost to sight. Although the council as a whole tried to convey the relationship between liturgy and life, the clarity that marked the first liturgical movement was not evident: that the liturgy of the Church shapes the faithful and the faithful contribute to the shaping of the world.

The failure to grasp that principle has meant that the very liturgy that Guéranger, Pius X, and Virgil Michel thought would forfend us against the spirit of the age has instead all too often succumbed to it. Instead of being an objective, communitarian rehearsal of our common identity, it becomes at times a stage for displays of individualism and subjectivism. As such it loses its authority and is there for us to make what we want of it.

It is perhaps easier to "catch" the difference between an objective and a subjective understanding of the liturgy than it is to define it. Some examples may help the process.

1) There was a funeral of a rather remarkable woman named Else who, after fleeing Nazi Germany, had become a Jungian counselor and had touched the lives of many. Her funeral was celebrated at an Anglican Benedictine abbey in the presence of friends and acquaintances from all sorts of different backgrounds. The ordinary was sung in

plainchant and several pieces of the Gregorian *Requiem* were also sung by the monks. Afterward a woman who, by her own admission, was not a churchgoer, disclosed that she had been profoundly moved by the liturgy, for, as she put it, the celebration of those ancient rites had the effect of taking up Else's life and incorporating it into the great transcendent stream of human life and history.

(2) By way of contrast there are wedding liturgies that only bear the slightest resemblance to the liturgy of the Church, with popular songs, personally meaningful readings and activities conceived by the couples themselves or by well-meaning friends or relatives. Although the traditional rites of Jewish and Christian marriage are full of images that serve to identify the couple who are marrying with figures who have gone before them, with Adam and Eve, Abraham and Sarah, Isaac and Rebeccah, Jacob and Rachel, these are omitted. A view of marriage as an institution and a tradition into which people enter and to whose constraints they must submit is far less common than it once was, and attempts are made to personalize and sometimes even improvise on the liturgy. The result is usually what was intended: a couple's wedding reflects them as individuals and as a couple, but sometimes nothing more.

Hence the dilemma this chapter has tried to pose by reviewing the two liturgical movements: Should we accommodate the liturgy to ourselves, encouraging a subjective approach to liturgy or engage in standing under the liturgy, regarding it in a more objective way? Perhaps we have had to work a number of things out of our systems to discover the shallowness of some of our earlier understandings and expectations, emerging with a real hunger for the life of the Spirit mediated by the liturgy, a life of the Spirit meant to change the face of the earth. To that end it perhaps would be helpful if we recaptured the earlier movement of liturgical reform, that which is more countercultural and yet more conscious of the world. Others seem to share this approach. Austin Fleming, for example, has proposed that instead of talking of "liturgy planning," we could talk of "preparation for liturgy," thereby shifting the focus from changing the rites to changing ourselves.[7] Perhaps instead of asking what will engage the assembly, we could begin to ask what the liturgy demands. Instead of asserting our ownership of the liturgy, we might ask how we can surrender to Christ's prayer and work. Instead of asking what we should choose to sing, perhaps we could start imaging how we might sing in such a way that it is no longer we who sing, but Christ who sings in us.

We stand at a crossroads. We must decide which way to go. Shall we continue to think of the liturgy as something to be adapted to our needs and tastes? Or move toward a liturgy that in its objectivity and givenness transcends the individuals who participate in it, lifting them up to engage in something far beyond their ability to create or even to imagine?

The rest of this book is an invitation to enter into "the very nature of the liturgy," its various levels and dimensions. It is a call to participate fully in the mysteries the liturgy holds "in earthen vessels," an image of what the great work of liturgy is all about with its power to make us who we are and our world all that it can be.

Notes

1. *Moto proprio* of Pius X, *Tra le sollecitudini* (November 22, 1903), trans. in *All Things in Christ: Encyclicals and Selected Documents of Saint Pius X*, Vincent A. Yzermans, ed. (Westminster, Md.: Newman, 1954) 200.

2. "The Liturgy, the Basis of Social Regeneration," *Orate Fratres* 9 (1935) 545.

3. "The Scope of the Liturgical Movement," *Orate Fratres* 10 (1936) 485.

4. Cf. *Sacrosanctum Concilium*: The Constitution on the Sacred Liturgy, Vatican Council II (1963) 21 (hereafter SC). (All quotations from Vatican II documents that are included in this book are taken from Walter M. Abbott, ed., *The Documents of Vatican II* [New York: The American Press, 1966].

5. SC 14.

6. SC 34.

7. *Preparing for Liturgy: A Theology and Spirituality* (Washington, D.C.: The Pastoral Press, 1985) 31–41.

2 Three Levels of Participation

As Virgil Michel saw, liturgy is a process by which we are taken up into something that transcends our individual lives and become involved in an enterprise that is far more than the sum of the efforts of the individual participants. The act of joining oneself to a larger enterprise is called "participation"; the act of joining oneself to the enterprise that is celebrated and effected in and through the Church's liturgy is called "liturgical participation." In this chapter, we shall explore some of the ritual and theological dimensions of the liturgy that might be important for understanding what it means to "participate" in the liturgy, and we shall try to glean from these reflections on the nature of liturgy some insight into what it means to participate fully.

Participation, after all, was the cornerstone of the postconciliar liturgical reform. According to the principle laid down by the council:

> Mother Church earnestly desires that all the faithful be led to that full, conscious, and active participation in the liturgical celebrations which is demanded by the very nature of the liturgy.[1]

I think it only fair to say that, by and large, English-speaking Catholics have conscientiously striven to be faithful to the council and to the wishes of the Church. New translations have been prepared, new music written, new hymnals published. The interior arrangements of churches have often undergone dramatic alteration. All of this was done in the name of "active participation," but was this precisely what was demanded "by the very nature of the liturgy"?

In English, "to participate" is a very active verb. Students are advised that their grade will depend in part upon their "classroom participation." Groups and organizations as diverse as parent-teacher organizations, political parties, and environmental groups spend a lot of time lamenting low levels of participation and discussing how to raise them. Conversely, while "participation" is generally considered a good thing, "non-participation"—whether it be in local elections, fund drives, or dances—is considered a bad thing, almost disloyal. Thus English-speaking Catholics, reading the liturgical text in light of cultural associations, have tended to perceive the move to encourage participation as a long overdue step toward democratizing the Church or as a way to keep modern people interested in what the Church has to offer. In either case, it could be seen as a concession to the marketplace in which the consumers want a more active say in what is going on, and are more likely to stay away out of boredom if not given the opportunity to "participate." Though there were undoubtedly some who saw more to the council's *actuosa participatio* than that, in most places "active participation" was simply understood as getting everyone to join in the responses and the singing and the moving about.

But was that in fact what Vatican II and the postconciliar reformers had in mind? Among the more significant passages of the liturgy constitution is the following:

> *By way of promoting active participation*, the people should be encouraged to take part by means of acclamations, responses, psalmody, antiphons and songs, as well as by actions, gestures, and bodily attitudes. And at the proper times all should observe a reverent silence.[2]

What is suggested here is that joining in the singing and the responses, the movements and the gestures, is less an end in itself than a means to whatever the council had in mind when it speaks of "active participation." Active participation is participation in something more than the ritual performance itself, but participation in what?

The council never explicitly defined what it meant by "participation," though the term has a long history in theology. Instead we are left to reconstruct what it might mean in this context from what the document says about the nature of the liturgy. On this topic, the opening paragraphs of the liturgy constitution have some rather fundamental things to say:

> [It] is through the liturgy, especially the divine Eucharistic Sacrifice, that the "work of our redemption is exercised." The liturgy is thus the outstanding means by which the faithful can express in their own lives, and manifest to others, the mystery of Christ and the real nature of the true Church. It is of the essence of the Church that she be both human and divine, visible yet invisibly endowed, eager to act and yet devoted to contemplation, present in the world and yet not at home in it. She is all

these things in such a way that in her the human is directed and subordinated to the divine, the visible likewise to the invisible, action to contemplation, and this present world to that city yet to come, which we seek. . . .[3]

In other words, the Church is sacramental in nature, in that its visible, human, and temporal dimension is meant to serve as the "outward sign" of the mystery of Christ that is its invisible, divine element recognized and recollected through the contemplative dimension of faith. This "Church-as-sacrament" is encountered most strikingly when the faithful assemble for the celebration of the liturgy. My thesis, then, is this: that the assembling and ritual performance of the local church is the human, visible, this-worldly dimension of the sign-sacrament Church and that full, conscious and active participation occurs when we so engage in the ritual celebration as to become engaged in the divine, invisible life of the world-to-come. In short, liturgy is symbolic from beginning to end. The realities it signifies—the mystery of Christ and the true nature of the Church—are attained in and through participation in the rites. But for this to happen, the rites have to be presented and understood as pointing to something beyond themselves. In other words, we need to take seriously and to manifest in the style of our celebrations the basic sacramentality of the whole rite.

In Catholic theology since the high Middle Ages, it has been customary to differentiate not two dimensions to the sacramental sign—the signifier and the signified—but three. It is difficult to explain this important point without having recourse to the Latin terminology, so perhaps we can set it out as follows:

1. The *sacramentum tantum* is the signifier taken on its own. It is the whole human, visible, ritual performance. To engage appropriately in the many different elements of that performance is to participate in the rite.

2. The *res et sacramentum* is what is immediately signified by the rite (but which also in turn signifies something more than itself). So, for example:

   the marriage ceremony is a signifier: it signifies two people getting married;

   the rite of baptism is a signifier: it signifies that the person baptized is becoming a member of the Church;

   the rite of ordination is a signifier: it signifies that someone who was not a priest is now a priest.

Note that in every instance, the ritual both signifies what is going on and makes it happen. What is signified and effected is a new social or ecclesial reality: a marriage, membership in the Church, being a priest. Of course, as we shall see, because the Church is not just any society but the Body of Christ, being a Christian couple, or a member of the Church, or a priest are specific identities, bringing unique rights and responsibilities specifically related to the mission of Christ and the Church, and which point to God and the saving reign of God. Nonetheless, to engage in the rite at this level, i.e., not just as ceremonial practice or play-acting, is to participate in a conventional action that has conventional effects, even if both the convention and its effects are peculiar to the Church.

3. The *res tantum* is what being baptized, or married, or ordained *ultimately* means. It is what all the signs finally point to: our union with God. This is often referred to as sanctifying grace, the gift of the Holy Spirit, the forgiveness of sins, love (*caritas*), or sharing the divine life. To engage in the rite at this level is to be open to the gift of God's own self and to participate in the very life of God, allowing the love that is of God and from God to fill our hearts and minds.

Each level of the sacrament involves a corresponding level of participation, governed by the constraints that are operative in the kind of performance or relationship appropriate at each level. To substantiate the thesis set out above, we must take a closer look at what is going on at each level in turn: the level of ritual, the level of the Christian economy, and the level of divine life.

LEVEL 1: PARTICIPATION IN RITUAL BEHAVIOR

At the first and most obvious level, available to any spectator who may drop in to observe a Christian liturgy, liturgy is ritual. Of course, the term "ritual" is a very broad one, being used to refer to a range of behavior extending from the courtship antics of the crested grebe to a presidential inauguration. Taken in this broad sense, it simply refers to behavior that is patterned, repetitive, and thus more or less predictable. Most of us have our own private rituals, such as those routines that enable us to negotiate the beginning and end of the day without having to think or make decisions, but the term "ritual" is perhaps more properly applied to all the different ways we learn to negotiate social interaction. Thus we have rituals of greeting and leave-taking, of table manners and commercial transactions. Above all, ritual is employed for those key moments in the life cycle—births, marriages, deaths—and in social life: graduations, legal transactions, governmental procedures. Rituals are pre-arranged patterns of behavior, sanctioned by convention if not by law, that govern human social interaction, especially on occasions fraught with anxiety, such as events of great personal or social importance.

The study of ritual has grown enormously in recent years thanks to the contributions of scholars working in a large number of different fields. The result is a plethora of complementary and often conflicting theories and insights. Here it will be sufficient to highlight four characteristics of ritual behavior that deserve to be recognized and acknowledged in liturgical celebrations.

Ritual Is Collective

The term "ritual" is properly applied to stereotyped forms of social interaction. It generally involves at least two persons, each playing their respective roles. Thus it takes two to apologize: one to make the apology, the other to receive it. On the other hand, it takes hundreds, if not thousands, to enact an inauguration: an incumbent, a chief justice, members of congress, party leaders, poets, musicians, guards. Moreover, it would be an odd inauguration if no one turned up to witness it, so any adequate account of the proceedings should probably include some reference to the invited guests and the crowds lining the presidential route.

As social interaction, then, and especially as an event with some sort of social consequences, ritual involves more than just the principals. And so it is with liturgy. From a ritual standpoint, liturgy is not the act of a presider alone but an enterprise involving a larger or smaller number of people, many of whom will have specific functions to perform.

Unlike a movie or theater audience, however, even the most passive assembly is not entirely passive. They will be engaged in some sort of performance, even if it is sometimes not strictly of a piece with the main performance or consistently in step with it. I have observed, for example, that those seated in the front pews of a church invariably join in the singing and in everything else. Those in the middle may or may not join in the singing, but they are likely to join in the responses and to stand up and sit down at appropriate times. Those in the back pews, however, are much more likely to read the bulletin than they are to join in the singing and the responses, but they will invariably stand up and sit down when it is appropriate to do so. Liturgy clearly allows for different degrees and levels of involvement, but (and because) it remains the action of the whole assembly. There are marked differences in the roles, scripted and unscripted, that people play, but the liturgy is the play and interplay of *all* the roles.

To study the liturgy, then, and to understand how it works, it is necessary to take into account the people who sit at the back as well as those who have seats in the sanctuary, those at the periphery as well as those at the center. This is perhaps more obvious to an anthropologist than to a theologian, for the theologian already knows what is significant and what is not. We have been taught for centuries to view the liturgy in terms of the sacramental "matter and form" and the "minister," and to regard the rest, whether it be the rite or the people, as dispensable. In reaction, there has been a tendency to insist on everyone's joining in practically everything. It is important, however, if we are to understand the true meaning of participation, to alter our focus and to recognize two things: first, the liturgy is the action of the assembled people as a whole; and second, not everyone is required to do everything at the same time.

Ritual Is Formal

The common denominator of all forms of ritual is that it is always more or less formal, always more or less predictable. Ritual is thus the opposite of spontaneous and original behavior. It calls for conformity rather than uniqueness, practice rather than inventiveness. It puts words into our mouths and assigns us roles to act out. At liturgy, this is as true for both the presider and the people in the back pew, the only difference being that the rules governing the presider's behavior are more compendious and more explicit than those regulating the others in the assembly.

We each have our part to play, and the whole undertaking is a communal event insofar as we each do what is expected of us, insofar as we observe the formalities.

Note that "what is expected of us" is both more and less than is written down in the *General Instruction of the Roman Missal*. Each local parish has its own way of doing things: its pattern for taking up the collection, its way of deciding who will bring up the gifts, its unique way of organizing the communion procession, its expectations about talking or not talking in church. We may not be able to articulate what all the rules are, but it only takes a visiting priest or a new liturgy coordinator to ignore the rules and we quickly become aware of them. The feelings of awkwardness, embarrassment, resentment, or anger aroused by the newcomer's deliberate or unwitting innovations give us a clue to the extent and importance of local ritual rules.

In fact, between the written rubrics of liturgical law and the unwritten patterns and expectations of local communities, there is really little leeway for improvisation. There is far less room, for example, for free and informal speech in the liturgy than most presiders realize, and most of that speech is assigned to the homilist. Certainly the presider can dispense himself from these constraints and make informal comments about the local sports scene or some other aspect of the parish agenda but only at the cost of alienating the very assembly he is trying to engage. The room for informal activity is even narrower than that for informal speech, and most of it is given to members of the assembly, who are freer to sit and read the parish bulletin or to get up and leave than are the ministers in the sanctuary.

Rituals function best when the formalities are observed. While ritual behavior may often be only vaguely defined and loosely prescribed, it tends nonetheless to be stereotyped and repetitive. Nothing in the *General Instruction of the Roman Missal*, for example, prescribes the speed or demeanor with which the ministers should make their way into the church, but there are certain parameters of "acceptable" behavior that can be broken by walking too fast or too slow or by grinning or glad-handing the members of the assembly on the way. Ritual is stereotyped and repetitive; it is a going through the motions. It is a kind of dance, in which the partners trust each other to do what they are supposed to do.

It would be a mistake, however, to think of ritual as something reserved for church and other formal occasions. Ritual pervades life, admitting of different degrees of formality in different contexts, ranging from morning greetings at the office to the more rigid protocols of law and diplomacy to the excruciatingly detailed and highly rehearsed prescriptions of such solemn events as inaugurations or installations. As these instances suggest, there is a rule at work here: the more solemn and portentous the event, the more invariant and rigid the procedures to be followed. Religion deals with matters of the greatest import, with questions of ultimate concern. Religion's rituals, therefore, tend to be prescribed with great exactness and to be highly predictable. They are marked by a certain weight and gravity, though they are not necessarily somber. They know the full range of moods and emotions, but their joy is as solemn as their sorrow. This is not to say that there is no room for the extraordinary, even for the ecstatic: only that there is no room for the flippant, the trivial, the jocose. It is their seriousness that supports their claim to be taken seriously. Trivializing the liturgy only undermines the confidence of the participants in the seriousness of activity in which they are engaged. Attempts to lighten up the liturgy slowly erode faith by drawing attention to the signifier and distracting from the signified. Liturgy is ritual: in order to function it requires the seriousness and reverence of which formality is the sign.

Ritual Is Performance

In his classic essay on "The Obvious Aspects of Ritual," the anthropologist Roy Rappaport accuses anthropologists (and his accusation applies *a fortiori* to theologians) of passing too quickly over the most obvious features of ritual behavior in order to try to decipher its meaning.[4] Although it may seem evident, it is worth saying that liturgy is first and foremost something that all believers are invited to *do*. It is a performance.

Although the word "performance" can easily engender thoughts of audiences watching performers, one observing the other at a distance, the use of the word here relies on its basic meaning, i.e., "to do something." Two points are worth making.

First, liturgy is something that is *done*. It does not exist in books, but comes to be at particular places and times as people get together to enact it. Liturgy's meaning is only realized in the doing. A theologian studying the texts of baptism tries to analyze the range of meanings that may be communicated when someone is actually baptized. But the text on the page is not a prayer; it becomes a prayer when hearts and voices enunciate it Godward. The rite of baptism can be discussed and analyzed, but baptism *happens* when, in a moment of ultimate seriousness, one person immerses another into the baptismal waters in the context of a community's tradition and its understanding of the consequences of doing so.

Put another way, liturgies are joint actions, carried out by the collaboration of individuals who play the part assigned to them. The meaning of the whole derives *not* from the personal interpretations or private intentions of the individual participants but from the social act itself. It is custom and convention that determine what this act means and what its consequences shall be. Liturgy is essentially a performance into which individuals fit themselves, discovering its meaning and implications as it were from the inside.

Second, liturgy is a performance that makes a difference. Ritual words and actions do not just express feelings: they make things happen. We tend to think of language as a medium for conveying information, for telling others what they do not know: "The new tax measure has been defeated in Congress," or "I'll be home late." But language serves many other purposes, and even when it conveys information, it is often doing something else as well: "It's raining" may be a way of saying "Take your umbrella"; the news that Carol has a headache may suggest that we ought to make allowances for her. In these instances, the telling makes a difference. Similarly, when I promise to see you tomorrow, I am not stating a fact but making a commitment.

Rituals are not just ways of communicating information or representing meaning: they also create new situations. Above all, they make a difference by creating, modifying, or sustaining *relationships*. Marriage rites, for example, are not only an expression of love: they marry people. The meaning of the rites derives from the rite, and individuals find meaning by submitting to the convention. Instead of simply expressing who they are, the rites also and more importantly redefine what they are. Participants, by participating, accept the (new) role given them by the rite—an act of role definition that can turn outsiders into insiders, strangers into brothers and sisters, the engaged into husband and wife, many individuals into one Body, and so on.

Liturgy makes a difference. Its efficacy is dependent, in the first place, on the conventions of the Christian community that celebrates it and whose tradition determines both the rules that govern correct performance and the social outcomes associated with such performances. To participate in the liturgy is to participate in an activity whose shape and meaning derive from a tradition and belongs to a community larger than the individual, larger even than the assembly gathered to celebrate. It is simply not true that the participants have to own the liturgy or to make it their own, in the sense of remodeling it to reflect their particular identity. On the contrary, they are to submit to it and let it give them an identity to grow into. For liturgy, like all ritual, is dependent for its effectiveness not just on the interior dispositions of the participants but on something prior to and largely independent of personal feelings and subjective authenticity, something which, far from mirroring our thoughts and feelings, instead confronts them.

That objective "something" that is bigger than all of us is, in the first place, something that embraces all of us. Emile Durkheim identified it with society itself, for what else transcends and embraces us all in the way our community or society does?[5] Durkheim has rightly been criticized for reducing the transcendent and the numinous to the experience of society, but in the case of the Christian liturgy his insight points us in the right direction. The liturgy undeniably belongs to and in some sense represents the universal Church and its tradition: the social efficacy of the rites depends on that. But in the case of the Church we are confronted with a society that is itself a sign of something other than, more than, greater than, itself: the "mystery of Christ."

Ritual Is Formative

To engage in ritual is to submit to its constraints, to assume the role allocated to us. This is true of the social rituals of celebrating a birthday, shopping for shoes or negotiating a bank loan as well as of the more solemn rites of marriage and death. It is also true of the weekly liturgy, where we are expected to stand and sit and kneel and bow and sign ourselves with the sign of the cross and carry candles and say certain words all at the appropriate time. To engage in ritual is to do what is expected of us. Liturgy, like all ritual, is a matter of convention and has a low tolerance for unconventional behavior.

Erving Goffman writes of the implicit social contract in terms of "framing." In any given situation or interaction, we instinctively register the clues as to what is going on and act accordingly. We act differently at home and in a restaurant, in conversation with a peer and in conversation with a government official, in discussing a personal problem and in debating a theoretical issue. In each case, the "frame" determines what speech and behavior is appropriate. Someone who misjudges the frame will act in ways that are embarrassing but forgivable; someone who deliberately breaks frame is likely to be resented and ostracized. Every situation is rule-governed, and every infraction of the rules will bring its own more or less explicit penalty, from being talked about behind one's back because of bad manners to being corrected for talking or smoking in a public library, to formal banishment for offenses against club rules, even to fines and prison sentences for breaking the rules established by society itself to regulate matters of public interest. Such rules, whatever their degree of formalization, serve to govern the forms of behavior conventional in our society for the establishment, maintenance, exercise and even restoration of relations between people, whether intimates or strangers.[6]

Liturgy is performance undertaken by a group of people together. It is a formal performance, in the sense that it consists of a number of forms of speech and set forms of behavior to which we are expected to conform. In short, ritual behavior is the opposite of spontaneous behavior, and the liturgy falls very definitely into the category of ritual behavior. Hard as it is for many of us to grasp, we are not free to make liturgy up as we go along but are required to carry it out, enact it, and perform it, so that it may form us.

Prayer in general and ritual prayer in particular is not a matter of externalizing inner thoughts and feelings but of maintaining a relationship with God in which we are committed to certain attitudes. For example, when we recite in the Creed, "I believe in God, the Father almighty . . . and in Jesus Christ, his only Son, our Lord. . . . I believe in the Holy Spirit," we are not reporting what we think but making an act of commitment to God—Father, Son, and Spirit. To be true or authentic, such a profession does not need to well up from an overflowing heart: it may be all the more authentic and valuable when uttered in the face of hopelessness, doubt and despair. Similarly, when the liturgy requires us to sing, "Glory to God in the highest and peace to his people on earth," it does not matter all that much whether or not we feel on top of the world. If we do, and the prayers and rites provide us with an outlet for expressing our mood and emotions, that's good; but if the ground does not shake and the heart does not quake, the exercise is not invalidated in the least. What matters is that we follow the indications of the rite and try to make its attitudes our own.

The liturgy, I would suggest, is the rehearsal or appropriate enactment of relationships: our relationship to God, to one another, to those who have gone before us, to those who will come after us, and to the world as a whole.

This view of liturgy as a rehearsal of relationships was brilliantly expressed in a sermon I heard years ago in Virginia Beach, Virginia. It was one of those Sundays in the summer when the gospel is the story of the multiplication of the loaves and fishes. Having read the gospel, the homilist began to talk about his experience of growing up in the

Chesapeake area in the 1940s. Apparently his family had lived there for several generations and various branches of the family were scattered around the same parish. On Sundays it was their custom to get together for dinner, an engagement so firm that it would never occur to a child to ask if he or she could go to the beach or the movies instead. The household that was to host the dinner on a given Sunday would go to the early liturgy and hasten home afterward to cook and bake and get the tables ready for the rest of the relatives who would come over after the later Eucharist. The children were always seated and fed first, whereupon the younger children were sent out in the yard to play while the older ones cleared the tables, washed the dishes and reset the table for the adults. When the adults finally sat down to eat, they settled in for the afternoon.

From time to time, the homilist recalled, the young children would come in and inquire whether it was time to go home yet, and it never was. All they could do was wait until they were old enough to be permitted to stay inside and wash the dishes and wait on the tables. And the older children, for their part, could always look forward to that glorious day in the future when they would be old enough to take their place at table with the adults. In the meantime, they did the fetching and the carrying, but they also did a lot of hanging around, observing how the adults behaved, listening in on adult conversations, overhearing the old stories, becoming accustomed to the way things were done at table in that family, so that when the time finally came for them to sit with the adults, they would know how to conduct themselves. And maybe, concluded the homilist, the reason why we are obliged to participate in the Eucharist every Sunday is to rehearse our table manners and to prepare to take our places with Abraham, Isaac and Jacob, and Ruth and Esther and Judith at the table in the kingdom of heaven.

To summarize this section on participation in ritual behavior, we can say that the liturgy of the Church is the kind of activity we classify as ritual. This classification enables us to see it as a collective undertaking and as an exercise of a convention, which means that participants are required to follow the rules and observe the constraints associated with the particular kind of ritual in question, so that it might be effective in defining or redefining the participants' roles. In this, liturgy is no different from other kinds of social convention and shares the characteristic features of civic and other kinds of ritual. Where it differs is in the nature of the community celebrating it for, while the Church is a society, a culture like any other, it differs from all others in claiming to point beyond itself to the mystery of Christ, i.e., to the mystery in which humankind encounters God. It is this unique characteristic of the Church that takes us to the second level of the sacramental sign and to the second level of participation.

LEVEL 2: PARTICIPATION IN THE LITURGY OF THE CHURCH AS THE WORK OF CHRIST

To understand that which makes Christian ritual unique, we must begin by looking to Christ himself. In the New Testament, such cultic terms as "priest," "sacrifice," "worship," and "liturgy" are used to refer not to Christian ritual but to Christ and his "obedience unto death" and secondly, to the ongoing life of the Christian community, lived in conformity to Christ (See Rom 12:1; 2 Cor 9:13; Rom 15:16[7]). The most "liturgical" of the New Testament writings, the Letter to the Hebrews, interprets the suffering and death of Jesus in light of the "sin offerings" of the temple and especially in light of the ritual on the Day of Atonement.

Consequently for our prayer to be acceptable, whether it be our public prayer or our private prayer, it must consist of our being drawn into a living participation in Christ's own sacrifice of obedience. For our prayer to be heard, it must be offered "in Christ," i.e., it must be one with the continuing prayer of Jesus himself as he endlessly glorifies the Father: "He holds his priesthood permanently, because he continues for ever. Consequently he is able for all time to save those who approach God through him, since he always lives to make intercession for them" (Heb 7:24-25). So the New Testament writers, in their different ways, evidence the conviction that there is only one priest (Christ) and only one liturgy (the paschal mystery) celebrated by our High Priest before the throne of God forever.

Genuine Christian prayer is prayer "in Christ." To say that Christ is the sole mediator between God and the human family is not to make him a go-between or a messenger. Christ is not between us and God but rather the place in which we stand before God. We come before God always and only as members of the Body of Christ, united with our head. To say we pray "in Christ" is to describe how we are present to God.

But it is always the head that prays, its prayer welling up from the depths of the heart of Christ, which is the heart of all humanity. That "welling up" of prayer is what we call "the Spirit," the Spirit at work in us making us one with Christ and through him, with God. That is why no prayer of ours can reach God unless we have that mind that was in Christ Jesus: unless our prayer is not only joined to his but is in fact *his* prayer welling up in us through our openness to his Spirit. That is why, ultimately, we never pray alone. My prayer is the prayer of all, the prayer of all is my prayer, because we are in Christ and Christ is in us all so that his prayer becomes ours and our prayer is his.

When we participate in the priestly functions of Christ in the liturgy, we do not address God directly or in our own name but "through Christ our Lord." We do not own the liturgy. Rather it is the liturgy of the whole Church that is given us by Christ as the means whereby we may enter into his liturgy. The difference between singing the *Gloria* in practice or in a concert, for example, and singing it in the liturgy, is that in the liturgy it becomes prayer, that is, the outward and audible form of that deeply inward and utterly inaudible prayer of the Spirit which is the prayer of Christ himself to God whom he called and taught us to call "Father."

So the first level of participation in the rite is subsumed into this second level of participation in the liturgy of Christ, which, however, is no ordinary ritual celebration but the endless self-giving of Christ into the hands of God from whom he receives back his life. His self-giving is the only form of worship worthy of and acceptable to God. Human worship that has any hope of being acceptable to God has to be the worship not of lips but of obedience: an offering of one's whole self, with and in Christ, to God. That is our participation in the paschal mystery of Christ's obedience unto death. Without that, we might as well stay in bed on Sunday morning; without that, all the praying and singing in the world is beside the point. So the second level of participation is identification with Christ in his radical obedience to God.

Let us turn now to the ecclesial dimension of this level of participation and reflect on two related issues: the identity of the Church as Body of Christ and the nature of faith.

The Church Is the Body of Christ

Familiar from the Pauline writings, the image of the Church as Body dominated people's understanding of the Church in the patristic and early medieval period when our liturgy largely took its shape. The image was subsequently eclipsed as emphasis shifted to the Church's institutional and organizational aspects and was only recovered in the nineteenth and twentieth centuries, when it became the underlying theology of the liturgical movement.

Body is a common metaphor for social entities in which many people work together to realize shared goals. We talk commonly enough about a "body" of people and the "body politic," while terms like "corps" and "corporation" (from the Latin *corpus*) carry the same metaphor into military and commercial life. But it is one metaphor that was found particularly apt when applied to the Church:

> There is one body and one Spirit, just as you were all called to the one hope of your calling, one Lord, one faith, one baptism, one God and Father of all, who is above all and through all and in all (Eph 4:4-6).

Body of Christ specifies the kind of body that the Church is. Christ is, first and foremost, the "Word made flesh" or "the human face of God." In the famous phrase coined by Edward Schillebeeckx, Christ is "the sacrament of our encounter with God."[8] Paul speaks of Christ as "the image of the invisible God" (Col 1:15), while in John's Gospel, when Philip asks Jesus to see the Father, Jesus replies, "Whoever has seen me has seen the Father"(John 14:9). In other words, the humanity of Jesus is the form of his divinity, the visible disclosure of the invisible God as here for us. As true God and true man, Jesus is the meeting place between God and humankind, between divinity and humanity, heaven and earth, time and eternity. But his interface is not static, not fixed and given once-for-all. On the contrary, his personality, his speech, his activity, represent an unfolding of the mystery of God in time and place, in history, on earth.

But, said Pope St. Leo I, "what was visible in the Lord has passed over into the mysteries (sacraments of the Church)."[9] The Church is the Body in which Christ continues to be present in history and to unfold the mystery of God among us. The Church is not a replacement for Christ but the mode of his visible presence in the world so that his mission of reconciliation—our reconciliation with God and with one another—might be carried forward.

The Meaning of Membership

Ritual performances, we have said, require the participants to play a role, act a part, assume an identity. In baptism Christians first assume their new identity; we are assigned to a role that will take a lifetime to grow into. Karl Rahner once suggested that we are all Christians in order to become Christians.[10] In baptism we become members of the Church, and we rehearse that role regularly in the celebration of the Eucharist. So what does it mean to become a member of the Church, the Body of Christ? We can best define it in terms of a new set of relationships to the world, the Church, and Christ.

Our relation to the *world* is changed. In baptism we pass from being outside the Church to being inside the Church. This does not mean a complete break with the world: we remain firmly rooted in our ecosystem and continue to live and work like the rest of the human race. But at the same time, we profess at baptism to take our values not from the world but from Christ; we renounce all values and beliefs alien to the Gospel. In so doing, we assume new responsibility for and to the larger world. The great prayer of the baptized, solemnly committed to them in the course of their initiation, teaches us to pray: "Thy kingdom come, thy will be done on earth as it is in heaven." In other words, we assume a responsibility to live in the world and for the world in such a way as to contribute to its transformation in accordance with God's will.

Our relationship to the *Church* is changed. Baptism makes us members of the Church, much as the ceremonies of naturalization make people from other lands into citizens of the country. With citizenship come certain inseparable rights (such as the right to vote) and responsibilities (such as to obey its laws). Similarly, Christian baptism is the source of certain rights and duties. Among the rights we must include the right to the sacraments and especially to the weekly Eucharist, the right to offer one's gift at the Eucharist, the right to assemble with other Christians, the right to regular and effective preaching, and the right to spiritual guidance. Among the corresponding duties we might name: bearing witness to the Christian life, assembling with the Church on the first day of the week, contributing to the Church's welfare according to one's abilities, sharing its mission to the poor, and supporting and challenging Church authorities.

Our relationship to *Christ* is also changed by baptism. The baptized become members of a community that defines itself in relation to Christ and receives its specific identity as a community from its relationship to Christ. That relationship, as we saw above, is more than one of love and loyalty; it is a relationship of representation, in which the Church is to represent Christ and to be the means whereby his redeeming work continues to unfold in history. This work of representing Christ is itself a further task of representation, since Christ is the representative of God. It can best be summed up as the double task of representing Christ to the world and the world to God. This does not make the Church a go-between, any more than Christ is a go-between between people and God. Rather, like Christ, the Church is to be the place where the timeless intersects with time, heaven and earth meet, and God and humanity embrace.

Thus baptism creates for those being baptized a new set of relationships to Christ, to the Church, and to the world. Anyone who is baptized, then, assumes the responsibility of taking part in representing God to the world and the world to God because this is the work of Christ that has passed over into the liturgy of the Church.

The Effects of Baptism

To push this line of thinking a little further, two additional remarks are in order. First, this new role or responsibility with which we are invested in baptism corresponds to what theologians since Augustine have called "character." The concept of sacramental character was invoked by Augustine in part to account for the non-repeatable nature of baptism and ordination, but it was subsequently obscured by speculations that identified it with some mark or quality of the soul. It was St. Thomas Aquinas who rescued the concept by defining character as "a certain kind of participation in the priesthood of Christ."[11] Given the liturgical practice of his time, it is hardly surprising that he distinguished between the active mode of participating in Christ's priesthood associated with the power of orders and the task of distributing the gifts of God, and the passive mode of participation, in which the laity were supposed merely to receive the grace of the sacraments. But if we understand the priesthood of Christ as related to his mediatorial and representative function and see the whole Church as his Body, as being invested with those same functions, then the baptismal "character" must mean the responsibility to contribute to the ongoing realization of Christ's role as mediator between God and humanity.[12]

The conferring of this mediatorial role is symbolized especially by the rites of baptism, confirmation, and orders, but all the sacraments and all liturgical rites of the Church have an ecclesial dimension proper to each and related more or less directly to this mediatorial function. Thus, marriage constitutes a couple as a new household of faith in which the love of Christ for his Church is to be made visible and in which the work of prayer, witness, and service is ongoing. In the anointing of the sick, the community, formally established with its priest as its head, represents the healing and saving mission of Christ to the sick and the suffering. In penance, the sacrament involves both the prayer of the Church on behalf of the sinner and the reintegration of the sinner into the priestly ministry of the whole Church. But it is above all in the Sunday Eucharist and in the public liturgy of the hours that this priestly work of representing God to the world and the world to God is accomplished.

Second, this new priestly identity is conferred automatically or, in traditional terms, *ex opere operato*, by virtue of a valid baptism and confirmation or a valid ordination. As long as we bear in mind that we are talking about social roles and responsibilities, there is no danger of treating this as magical. It simply means that, as we saw, liturgy is a form of ritual and ritual is performative: it negotiates relationships and confers identity.

To say that sacraments work *ex opere operato* is simply to say that they operate as other rituals do, as conventional procedures entailing conventional consequences. And their conventional force suffers the same limitations as all other conventions. They can change our status, but *as conventions* they cannot make us better people. Naturalization can make me a citizen, but it cannot make me loyal. Marriage can make a married man of me, but it cannot make me a loving spouse. The rite of ordination can make someone a priest, but it cannot make that person holy or competent. On the other hand, the common expectation is that new citizens should love their new country, that priests should be religious leaders, that newlyweds should care about each other. In other words, we expect that the relationship should in each case be more than purely formal or juridical. It should be, we might say, *real*! And the expectation is justified on grounds connected with the ritual itself, for while the rite cannot itself create the appropriate frame of mind it usually *implies* such a frame of mind or disposition.

And so it is with all the sacraments and the liturgy as a whole. Participation in the ritual performance has certain socio-ecclesial entailments—one has fulfilled one's obligation, been absolved or baptized or ordained or married—but participation that went no further would rightly be felt to fall short, to be mere formalism. Since that participation is participation in a formal act of the Church-as-sacrament and not just play-acting, it signifies and thus implies a relationship with God in faith.

The Nature of Faith

Reacting against too conceptual an understanding of faith that tended to identify it with belief, and wanting to recover the broader sense in which "faith" is used in the Scriptures, the Dogmatic Constitution on Divine Revelation availed itself of the Pauline term, "the obedience of faith":

> "The obedience of faith" must be given to God who reveals, an obedience by which a man entrusts his whole self freely to God, offering "the full submission of intellect and will to God who reveals," and freely assenting to the truth revealed by him.[13]

Thus, while citing Vatican Council I in order to express continuity with the teaching of that council, Vatican II goes back to St. Paul (Rom 16:26; cf. Rom 1:5; 2 Cor 10:5-6) to redress the cognitive approach of nineteenth-century Catholicism by giving priority to faith as entrusting oneself wholly and entirely to God.

The Belgian theologian Piet Fransen put it this way:

> By "faith" the New Testament expressed the free and definitive dedication of our life to Christ in the unconditional acceptance of His message of redemption . . . and of the way of life exemplified in himself. . . .[14]

Coming at the matter from an entirely different angle, that of a developmental psychologist, James Fowler has highlighted the volitional and trusting dimensions of faith in claiming that faith is not an exclusively religious phenomenon:

> Rather, faith becomes the designation for a way of leaning into life. It points to a way of making sense of one's existence. It denotes a way of giving order and coherence to the force-field of life. It speaks of the investment of life-grounding trust and life-orienting commitment.[15]

Seen in this way, the issue is not that believers have faith and unbelievers do not but that every human being has to have some way of making sense of the buzzing confusion of human experience, something that they ultimately rely on, something that helps them get by in life. Faith, in this sense, is a universal phenomenon, and people who are searching for it are not people who have never had it but people who have lost faith in that which they previously put their faith. The question that counts for the Christian, therefore, is not whether a person has faith or not, but whether their life-grounding trust and life-orienting commitment is invested in the God and Father of Jesus Christ or elsewhere: a question that applies as much to the practicing Catholic as anyone else.

Simply put, I want to suggest that Christian faith exists in three dimensions. The faith that saves has to be *our* faith, but our faith has to be *the faith of the Church*, and the faith of the Church has to be *the faith of Christ*. The sense of this suggestion may become clearer if, for "faith," we read "life-grounding trust," "life-orienting commitment," or "the obedience of faith." The "obedience" of the believer is a participation in the obedience of the Church, but the obedience of the Church is meaningless apart from the Church's participation in the obedience of Christ. There is, in short, only one faith: one Lord, one faith, one baptism (Eph 4:5). Any faith that is a saving faith is a participation in, and personal appropriation of, that one faith.

The Faith of Christ

The Scriptures do not usually attribute faith to Christ (though the Epistle to the Hebrews speaks of him as "the pioneer and perfecter of our faith" [Heb 12:2]) and it sounds distinctly odd in the Catholic tradition to speak of Jesus as having faith. Yet if faith is defined as "life-grounding trust and life-orienting commitment" or, in the more biblical language, as "obedience," then clearly faith and faithfulness are what most decisively characterize the life and death of Jesus. John speaks of Jesus as doing the will of him who sent him (John 4:34ff.). The Synoptics tell the same story, most explicitly perhaps in the prayer of Jesus in the Garden of Olives. The Epistle to the Hebrews makes the point repeatedly:

> [He] was faithful to the one who appointed him [as our high priest], just as Moses also "was faithful in all God's house" (3:2).

And again:

> In the days of his flesh, Jesus offered up prayers and supplications, with loud cries and tears, to the one who was able to save him from death, and he was heard because of his reverent submission. Although he was a Son, he learned obedience through what he suffered; and having been made perfect, he became the source of eternal salvation for all who obey him (5:7-9).

So salvation is to be found in obedience and submission through the obedience of faith offered to God, who alone can save us out of death. By his own faith, Jesus became the source of salvation to all who obey (i.e., put their faith in) him. The faith of Jesus was manifest in his obedience

> . . . to the point of death,
>   even death on a cross.
> Therefore, God also highly exalted him
>   and gave him the name
>   that is above every other name,
> so that at the name of Jesus
>   every knee should bend,
>   in heaven and on earth and under the earth,
> and every tongue should confess
>   that Jesus Christ is Lord,
>   to the glory of God the Father."
>   (Phil 2:8-11)

Thus God is attested and glorified by the faith life of Jesus. God in turn glorifies him and attests to him, establishing him in his exaltation as the source of salvation for all who follow the Son in obedience or submission to God.

The Faith of the Church

The faith of the Church does not consist of using right language: "Why do you call me 'Lord, Lord,' and do not do what I tell you? I will show you what someone is like who comes to me, hears my words, and acts on them. That one is like a man building a house, who dug deeply and laid the foundation on rock. . . ." (Luke 6:46-48).

The faith of the Church, therefore, is not just what it professes to believe. It is, fundamentally, its characteristic way of "leaning into life." The faith of the Church is more than any doctrine, more than anything the Church can say. Ultimately, it is what the Church does in obedience to Christ and in conformity to the pattern of his own life, death, and resurrection. In brief, the faith of the Church is the faith of Christ: it is that existential subordination of itself to God which is the fruit of assimilating the Spirit of Christ and thus reproducing in this historical collective that same mind which was in Christ Jesus. Christ's own obedience of faith is the rock on which the Church is built, beginning with the apostles whose deaths so closely imitated that of their Master. From then until now, the Church has found and continues to find its identity in its commitment to discovering and submitting to God's will and to carrying it out in the world. In this way, the Church, in being obedient to Christ, participates in Christ's obedience to God.

Thus God, whose love and mercy were displayed and glorified when Jesus entrusted his life into God's hands, continues to be glorified when the Church, by its faith and obedience, gives new scope for the manifestation and glorification of God's will to save. Hence liturgy is only one of the ways in which the life of the Church gives glory to God, and it remains hollow and dishonest it if is not at the same time an act of collective faith and obedient submission to God.

The Faith of the Participant

The Council of Trent summed up centuries of Christian teaching when it declared that the sacraments confer grace on anyone who does not put an obstacle in the way. This teaching, expressed in negative terms because of the attempt to counter the Reformers, especially Luther, can be expressed positively: the sacraments are the means whereby those who entrust themselves to God are drawn into the divine life.

The sacraments require faith—the obedience whereby we entrust our whole selves freely to God—if they are to achieve their purpose fully, if they are to "confer grace." The liturgy does not glorify God or save us without our faith. God calls us to respond wholeheartedly, each of us according to our capacity to act freely. The effect of such faith-filled, or self-abnegating, liturgical participation is a growing trust, a growing freedom, and hence a growing faith. No one can fruitfully participate in the liturgy without a minimum of faith or trusting self-surrender and thus without some measure of Christ's self-abandonment to the One who alone could save him out of death.

In conclusion, the move from the visible to the invisible, from the human to the Christian dimension of the liturgy, requires faith. This we defined, following Vatican II and the New Testament, as obedient submission: the obedience whereby a person entrusts his or her whole self freely to God. To participate in the rite with that kind of self-emptying is to participate in the priestly work of Christ and to render visible and tangible here and now the eternal liturgy that Christ himself celebrates before the throne of God. We are baptized into the Church, Christ's Body, in order to participate in his mediatorial role and continue his work on this earth until the day that God becomes "all in all." We now move to the third level of participation that foreshadows that parousial moment.

LEVEL 3: PARTICIPATION IN THE LIFE OF GOD

Catholic theologians since Augustine have customarily distinguished two sets of effects resulting from the sacraments. There is the *res et sacramentum* or *character*, which we have just described as the ritual or socio-ecclesial effect and identified as a commission to participate in the priestly function of Christ himself. But because the socio-ecclesial effect is precisely an assimilation to Christ in his mediatorial role, it implies a further level of reality: our relationship with God in Christ. This is called "grace" or "sanctifying grace" or "gift of the Holy Spirit" and constitutes the *res tantum* of the liturgy: that which is ultimately signified and which itself signifies nothing beyond itself.

Ideally they go together, the *res et sacramentum* and the *res tantum*. Ideally, participation in the Eucharist will mean that "we who are nourished by this body and blood [will] be filled with his Holy Spirit and become one body, one Spirit in Christ" (Eucharistic Prayer III). But this may not happen always for everyone. The organist may be so focused on the music that she never gets beyond the level of a purely musical performance. The presider may be so focused on the need to communicate with the assembly that he never actually communicates in any engaged way with God. A couple may be so areligious that all their attention is focused on each other and on "their day" that their marriage, though celebrated in church, is ultimately a secular affair: a sacrament but not an event of grace, valid, as the theologians and canonists say, but not fruitful. The ritual has its socio-ecclesial effect, but the people described here are not open to mediating God's presence in the world.

To be itself a credible sign, the liturgical assembly must be more than just the Church on duty; it has to be a community that can be taken seriously as witnessing to the living God and holding out hope for humanity. This is why, particularly in the thinking of Paul VI, Mary is the model of the Church. She not only listened to the word, heard the word, took it to heart, but allowed the Word to become flesh in her. By her "fiat," she herself became absorbed by and transparent to God's self-communication to the human race. Citing Irenaeus, the council taught that Mary "being obedient, became the cause of salvation for herself and for the whole human race."[16] What permitted God to act in and through her was that she was not merely passive but co-operated actively in the work of redemption "through free faith and obedience."[17] Her openness, her attentiveness, her welcoming of the Word, allowed God to communicate with the world. So it is with the Church at large and with the local parish. Our function—our vocation—

is to cooperate in the mediating work of Christ as links between God and the human world. For that ritual is indispensable, but it is never enough. For that we need holiness, in the sense of a certain Christ-like transparency to the Spirit of God. That openness to God is what we call faith; that transforming self-gift of God to us we call sanctifying grace.

But St. Thomas Aquinas defined sanctifying grace as a certain participation in the life of God,[18] i.e., the *third* level of participation. Ultimately then, full, conscious, and active participation in the liturgy of the Church means nothing less than full, conscious, active participation in the life of grace, lived and manifested individually and collectively, as union with God and communion with all humanity.

Participation in the life of God is a mystery ultimately beyond telling, but we have to say that it is participation in the communitarian life of God. This is the life of which the One we have been privileged by baptism to call "Father" is the inexhaustible course: the God who is source and end of all created things. It is life lived as sons and daughters in the Son, the Word who was begotten of the Father from all eternity and is forever of one being with the Father. It is life whose very form is the Spirit of the Holy God, poured into our hearts, flooding their depths, to draw us into the depths of God. As Irenaeus wrote nearly eighteen centuries ago:

> Those who receive the Spirit of God are led to the Word, that is,
>   to the Son;
> but the Son receives them and presents them to the Father;
> and the Father bestows incorruptibility on them.
> So, without the Spirit no one can see the Word of God,
> and without the Son no one can approach the Father,
> for the Son is knowledge of the Father,
> but knowledge of the Son is through the Holy Spirit.[19]

Participation in God

In the 1960s when the first official English texts were being prepared for liturgical use, the translators struggled with the semantic density and syntactic conciseness of the original Latin collects. One of the problems they had was with the fact that almost every collect began with the word *"Deus"* ("God") or the phrase *"omnipotens, sempiterne Deus"* ("Almighty, everlasting God"). To many, these addresses seemed both bald and distant, so in some countries' translations they were often changed to "Father." Certainly this had the effect of making

God more personal to us, and it invoked the baptismal relationship that is at the source of our ability to address God at all. Unfortunately, however, with the rise of feminist consciousness, the improvement turned out to be highly ambivalent, especially given its frequency in eucharistic formularies. On the other hand, it is precisely God-as-source-and-end-of-all-things, the One from whom all life proceeds and to whom all life returns, who is addressed, praised, thanked, and invoked in the liturgy of the Church. How do we begin to name this endless mystery of the love we believe to pulse at the heart of the universe?

The names of God are many because none of them is adequate. The danger of them all is that they be mistaken for the real name, the definable identity of the One who, when asked for a name, would only tell Moses: "I am who I am" (Exod 3:14) (itself only one of several ways in which the sacred tetragram YHWH can be read). What must be remembered, then, as we ease into the familiar words and ways of our rites, is that in the liturgy we stand before God and that to do so is to stand before the Mystery, to stand on the edge of an abyss, on the edge of language, on the edge of knowing. To pray is to hurl words into the vast infinity of the silent mystery of God, but often we rattle them off as if we were shelling peas, and they come pinging back to us, failing to penetrate beyond the sphere of our self-absorption. We know we have prayed only when we cannot remember what we were saying, when the nakedness of our exposure to God or the urgency of the spirit of prayer makes our spirit leap in God's Spirit and transcend what we can contain in words.

The practice of saying prayers, including liturgical prayers, must keep the mystery of God before us and not allow God to become reduced to a handy-dandy, pocket-sized deity or a convenient friend in the sky. The language of public prayer is closer to the language of the poet than that of the theologian, and it needs to be read that way.

> O world invisible, we view thee.
> O world intangible, we touch thee.
> O world unknowable, we know thee.
> Inapprehensible, we clutch thee.[20]

Assembling for the liturgy, celebrating the hours and sacraments of the Church, is a calculated act of self-exposure at the edge of abyss. The role of the sacraments is not to deliver God to us, not to package the One whom the world cannot contain, not to "confer" grace, but to

deliver us to the place where God can be God for us. God does not fall
into our hands, but Scripture warns us that "it is a fearful thing to fall
into the hands of the living God" (Heb 10:31). It is a fearful thing, not
because God is not merciful and compassionate but because to risk
knowing God is to risk knowing ourselves. To know the holiness of God
is to know our own unholiness as finite, guilty creatures, called ultimately to struggle, to suffer, and to die. Against this painful recognition,
we protest our good intentions, our respectfulness, our good works,
clinging to the tattered illusions of self-worth. But in the end there is
death, the limit that shadows and underlines all other limitations: death,
where we lose everything we have left to lose. Liturgy would deliver us
from this futile and self-defeating campaign of self-justification by offering us an alternative: that of dropping the illusions we cling to, rehearsing the trust that will enable us to let go in the end to life itself and
to surrender ourselves one last time into the hands of the living God.

Because liturgy *is* ritual, the role of the pastoral liturgist will certainly include attending to the details of the celebration. Because
liturgy is mundane, ordinary, routine, and familiar, the pastoral liturgist's work will also involve a lot of mundane, ordinary, routine, and familiar tasks, from choir rehearsals to training readers and servers, to
cleaning up after the liturgy has ended. But since the liturgy is sacramental, a sign and embodiment of the holy, the pastoral liturgist's role
also has another dimension: preparing a people, a time and a place for
exposure to the mystery of God:

> O world invisible, we view thee.
> O world invisible, we touch thee.[21]

Pastoral liturgists should think of themselves as "keepers of the fire"
or "guardians of the sacred threshold." Only reverence, a profound respect for the mysteries, a deep sense of what is holy, a hunger for the
true and the beautiful, can enable them to accompany others to the
threshold or to keep the fire alight.

Participation in Christ

It is a fundamental but rarely mentioned truth of the Catholic faith
that no one can have access to God except in and through Christ.
When this is discussed at all, it is usually in the context of questions
about the possibility of salvation outside the Church, but the same
conviction comes into play when we think about the life of grace or

the act of prayer. To be in grace (inside or outside the Church) is to be in some sense assimilated to, or incorporated into, Christ by the working of the Spirit. Our unity with one another, the unity that ultimately matters, is our natural solidarity as human beings sharing the same human condition and our new solidarity in the Spirit whereby we are sharers in the divine condition.

In thinking of Christ's mediatorial role, therefore, we should not think of Christ as coming *between* us and God, as a go-between accentuating our continuing distance from God even as he bridges it. Rather we come to God *in* Christ, where Christ is the holy ground, the very place of encounter, the way into the abyss of the mystery of God. Christ proclaimed himself to be "the way, and the truth, and the life. No one comes to the Father except through me" (John 14:6). He is Jacob's ladder: "Very truly I tell you, you will see heaven opened and the angels of God ascending and descending upon the Son of Man" (John 1:51). As the image suggests, a ladder is for descending as well as for ascending, and it invites us to descend first into death, into loss. "Do you not know that all of us who have been baptized into Christ Jesus were baptized into his death? Therefore we have been buried with him by baptism into death, so that, just as Christ was raised from the dead by the glory of the Father, so we too might walk in newness of life" (Rom 6:3-4). The pattern of Christ's life and death is the expression (in the form of a human life) of the Son's relationship to the Father. It is the pattern of our own approach to God: the journey of a lifetime but recapitulated, rehearsed, and advanced whenever we come to the liturgy. "O come, let us worship and bow down, let us kneel before the Lord, our Maker! For he is our God, and we are the people of his pasture, and the sheep of his hand" (Ps 95:6-7).

The paschal mystery is the entrusting of one's life to God, who alone can save us out of death, in solidarity with Christ. What we call "created grace" is the transformation of human beings, singly and together, into credible witnesses to God, which comes about through their assimilation to Christ, in whose face shines the glory of God. In the words of the early Christian doxology: "Glory be *to* the Father, *through* the Son, *in* the Holy Spirit in the holy Church. Amen."

Participation in the Spirit

The final phrase of the doxology suggests rather well how this access to God (which does not occur without changing us) occurs: "in the Holy Spirit in the holy Church." Our life in Christ, lived before God, is the work of the Spirit of God. "Spirit" is the name of the bond that links the Father and the Son from all eternity, and it is this same creative Spirit of love that hovered over the chaos in the beginning of creation and that now transforms the broken shards of our humanity into a new creation. It is this same Spirit that brings us together in Christ and in Christ brings us together in God.

Thus the Spirit may be thought of as the principle of relatedness. It was the Spirit that brought together the Word of God and the flesh of the human condition in the Incarnation, for Jesus "was conceived by the Holy Spirit and born of the Virgin Mary." The same reality was given new symbolic expression at the baptism of Jesus, when the Spirit descended on him at the Jordan and revealed him to be the Anointed of God. Through this double anointing with the Spirit, Jesus is seen to be related to the invisible God, indeed to be the presence of God among us in human form. At Pentecost (or on Easter Sunday, according to the Gospel of John), this same Spirit was poured out on the community of Jesus' disciples to make them "one Body, one Spirit in Christ," united to God and to one another. Thus participation in the life of God is a participation in the communitarian life of Father, Son and Spirit.

In short, the liturgy of baptism assigns us a new identity. On the most basic level it admits us to the rituals of the Church, but even more than that, it assigns us a new role, namely, participants in Christ's priestly function of representing God to the world and the world to God. But this responsibility can only be fulfilled with the grace of the Holy Spirit, for the Spirit creates in our hearts the real sense of solidarity with our fellow human beings and with the mystery of God-in-Christ, which the carrying out of such a commission presupposes. In this way the three levels of participation—in the rite, in the priesthood of Christ, in the life of God—belong together, and together they constitute that "full, conscious and active participation" in the liturgy that has always been integral to the Christian life and that the council sought to facilitate through its general reform of the liturgy.

Participation in History

One of the weaknesses of traditional ways of talking about liturgy and sacraments has been its focus on the individual's transformation and general neglect of the communitarian aspect, the fact that the Church and the larger world are in process of transformation through the sacramental-liturgical life of the People of God. The human race, and especially though not exclusively those of us who are believers, are in process of being changed: "And all of us, with unveiled faces, seeing the glory of the Lord as through reflected in a mirror, are being transformed into the same image from one degree of glory to another; for this comes from the Lord, the Spirit" (2 Cor 3:18).

In other words, the transformation of the human race into the image of Christ, which restores what was lost by sin, our original likeness to God (Gen 1:27), occurs by degrees over the whole course of history. It takes time to happen, and its happening gives time its meaning and purpose. In the course of time, Jesus is in process of becoming Christ, as his Body grows and the Divine finds more and more scope in human lives. God is in process of becoming God, as God is God for us. Jesus is becoming Christ, God is becoming God, insofar as we by our "free faith and obedience" permit the Spirit to transform us into the human likeness of God, so that God can be all in all.

This is what the Latins call "sanctification" and the Greeks call "divinization," and it occurs in history, over the course of centuries, as God gathers a people "from age to age" in Christ. Recognizing this historical dimension to the mystery of salvation, St. Thomas Aquinas identified three distinct but connected dimensions to the liturgy:

1. There is the *past of God's already accomplished acts*, above all the events of Christ's life, death, and resurrection, which in the liturgy we recall and celebrate as the source of our life with God.
2. There is *the future which we anticipate in the liturgy* and which to some extent we already enjoy in the liturgical assembly: the future when all God's people are gathered in and God is all in all.
3. There is *the present* in which the God who was revealed in past events, especially in the history of Israel and in the Christ, comes close to us in the Spirit to transform us into what we are yet to be.[22]

Where the Eucharist is concerned, St. Thomas compacted his theology of history into a brief antiphon found in his *O Sacrum Convivium*, the Office of the feast of Corpus Christi:

> O sacred banquet, in which Christ is eaten, the memory of his
> passion is recalled, the mind is filled with grace and we are given
> a pledge of the glory to be.

So the eucharistic liturgy is a commemoration of Christ's saving death and resurrection ("passion") in the past, and a foretaste of the heavenly banquet to come. In the meantime, we are in transition between that past and that future, as the grace of the sacramental eating and drinking provides not only a link to the past but a guarantee of the future.

CONCLUSION

This has been a rather lengthy excursion around the front and back sides of the liturgy. It was intended not so much as an exhaustive description of how and what the rites signify than as a taking of bearings.

On the front side, the obvious side, is the gathered assembly and its ritual performance. On the hind side is the mystery of the invisible God. Between the two is the mystery of the Church as Body of Christ. The challenge in liturgical practice is to know how to move from the visible to the invisible, from the human to the divine, from the signifier to the signified. For this, the key word is "participation."

"Participation," it now appears, means much more than getting the assembly to appear more involved. It means:

1. participating in the *rite* as a whole according to one's assigned role and doing so in such a way that one is
2. participating in the *priestly work of Christ* on behalf of the world before the throne of God and thus identifying with Christ dead and risen; and
3. participating in the *trinitarian life of God* as human beings.

In so doing, we are also participating in God's work in human history, which leads very quickly to the realization that true liturgical participation must have social and political consequences. To that we shall return, but first we need to explore at greater depth what it means to participate in the rite "in such a way" that all three levels of participation are attained in relative simultaneity.

Notes

1. SC 14.
2. SC 30 (emphasis added).
3. SC 2.
4. "The Obvious Aspects of Ritual," in *Ecology, Meaning and Religion* 2nd ed. (Richmond, Calif.: North Atlantic Books, 1979) 173–221.
5. *The Elementary Forms of the Religious Life*, trans. Joseph Ward Swain (London: George Allen & Unwin Ltd., 1915) 59ff.

6. See Erving Goffman, *Frame Analysis: An Essay on the Organization of Experience* (Cambridge, Mass.: Harvard University Press, 1974).

7. Biblical references and quotations are taken from the *New Revised Standard Version.*

8. *See* Edward Schillebeeckx, *Christ the Sacrament of the Encounter with God* (Kansas City: Sheed & Ward, 1963).

9. St. Leo the Great, *Serm.* 74(2), *De Ascensione Domini* II 2 (J.P. Migne, *Patrologiae cursus completes,* Series Latina [Paris-Montrouge, 1844–1864] 54:398).

10. *Foundations of Christian Faith: An Introduction to the Idea of Christianity,* trans. William V. Dych (New York: The Seabury Press, 1978) 407. Specifically, Karl Rahner wrote: "The crucial struggle involved in moral striving is not of course denied or trivialized by the fact that a person really becomes a Christian by accepting himself as the person he really is. . . . Nor is this struggle denied or trivialized by the fact that he becomes a person for the first time by accepting himself as a person in order to be a Christian."

11. *Summa Theologiae,* III, 63, 3, trans. David Bourke (New York: McGraw-Hill Book Co., et al., 1975).

12. It would take us too far astray to explore whether the "character" of confirmation differs in any substantial way from that of baptism, so I am combining the two as "baptismal character." On the other hand, the sacrament of orders would seem to invest individuals within the community with special responsibility for exercising this "priestly" or "representative" function with the Church to all the baptized, representing God to the Church and the Church to God *in persona Christi.*

13. *Dei Verbum:* Dogmatic Constitution on Divine Revelation, Vatican Council II (1965) 5 (citations omitted; hereafter DV).

14. *Intelligent Theology,* vol. 1 (London: Darton, Longman & Todd, 1967) 127.

15. "Perspectives on the Family from the Standpoint of Faith Development Theology," *Perkins Journal* (Fall 1979) 7.

16. *Lumen Gentium:* Dogmatic Constitution on the Church, Vatican Council II (1964) 56, citing *Adv. haer.,* III, 22,4: *PG* 7, 959, A (Harvey, 2, 123) (hereafter LG).

17. LG 56.

18. *Summa Theologiae,* IaIIæ, 3, 5, trans. Cornelius Ernst (New York: McGraw-Hill Book Co., et al., 1972).

19. Démonstration 7, translated from *Démonstration de la Prédication apostolique,* ed. Léon-Marie Froidevaux, *Sources chrétiennes* 62 (Paris: Cerf, 1959).

20. Francis Thompson, "The Kingdom of God," ed. Terence L. Connolly, *Poems of Francis Thompson,* rev. ed. (New York: Appleton-Century Co., 1941) 293.

21. Ibid.

22. *Summa Theologiae,* III, 60,3, trans. David Bourke (New York: McGraw-Hill Book Co., et al., 1975).

3 The Inward/Contemplative Dimension of Liturgy

In April 1964, just a few months after the solemn promulgation of the Constitution on the Sacred Liturgy and just as the first changes in the eucharistic liturgy were beginning to appear, the aging and by then ailing liturgist-theologian Romano Guardini wrote an open letter to the Liturgical Congress being held at Mainz in Germany. At a time when everyone else was apparently riding a wave of enthusiasm over the prospect of changes to come, Guardini sounded a note of caution. To many of his contemporaries it sounded sour and out of tune with the times; forty years later it sounds prophetic:

> Liturgical work, as we all know, has reached an important juncture. The Council has laid the foundations for the future. . . . But now the question arises how we are to set about our task, so that truth may become reality.
>
> A mass of ritual and textual problems will, of course, present themselves—and long experience has shown how much scope there is for a right and a wrong approach. But the central problem seems to me to be something else: the problem of the cult act or, to be more precise, the liturgical act.[1]

Guardini then went on to hint at what he meant by "the liturgical act":

> As I see it, typical nineteenth-century man was no longer able to perform this act; in fact he was unaware of its existence. Religious conduct was to him an individual inward matter which in the "liturgy" took on the character of an official, public ceremonial. But the sense of the liturgical action was thereby lost. The faithful did not perform a proper liturgical act at all, it was simply a private and inward act, surrounded by ceremonial and not infrequently accompanied by a feeling that the ceremonial was really a disturbing factor.[2]

Guardini's letter is full of important insights and hard questions, but he did not actually define what he meant by "the liturgical act." Apparently, it is a human act, i.e., something that had once been done with a certain self-conscious intentionality, but which had gradually atrophied and been converted into something else over the course of centuries. As a result of cultural changes and the consequent changes in religious mentalities, religious behavior had taken on different meanings. The end result was an understanding of religion that sees it primarily in terms of the individual (what the individual does with his solitude, as William James defined religion[3]) and makes interiority the sole criterion of authenticity. Such a starting point would inevitably tend to regard public and collective demonstrations of religiosity with suspicion and, even in the Catholic tradition, to dismiss "ceremonies" as a potential distraction from real prayer or at best as a kind of adjunct to and support for personal piety.

Perhaps envisaging that not only opponents of the liturgical changes, but even some who enthusiastically adopted and implemented the changes might be people whose outlook and spirituality were quite remote from those of the early centuries who had formed the liturgy, Guardini added:

> The question is whether the wonderful opportunities now open to the liturgy will achieve their full realization; whether we shall be satisfied with just removing anomalies, taking new situations into account, giving better instruction on the meaning of ceremonies and liturgical vessels or whether we shall relearn a forgotten way of doing things and recapture lost attitudes.[4]

By "lost attitudes" and "a forgotten way of doing things" he seems to suggest a way of approaching the liturgy and engaging in its sights and sounds, its words and gestures, that had been eclipsed by the rise of individualism and the split between inner and outer dimensions of the self. The "lost attitudes" would not see true prayer in "private and inward" terms, and would not see the public, communitarian performance of liturgy as serving only a ceremonial function. To put the matter in positive terms, these "lost attitudes" seem to consist in seeing the liturgy as constituted essentially by "participation," i.e., by participation in something of the sense in which we developed it in the last chapters. The "forgotten way of doing things" was not just turning the presider around to face the people or restoring the offertory procession, congregational song, or any of the other now restored practices that had disappeared over the centuries. Rather, what had been forgotten was the secret of how to participate in liturgy, I would propose, not just at one level but at all three levels of participation simultaneously.

The liturgy of the Church communicates in signs of every kind, in the languages of space and time; in roles, gestures, postures and processions; in speech and song, prose and poetry; in the sight and touch of sacred objects, in the smells of balsam and incense; in the colors of vestments and paraments, in lights and flowers, in icons and statues. There is hardly a form of symbolic communication that the liturgy does not employ, and each of these forms is open to understanding at all three levels of participation. Even though it would probably not be humanly possible, attending to all of them would constitute the fullest, most conscious, and most active participation possible in the liturgical event. Even to attend to some of them at any given liturgy would promote participation in the inward or contemplative dimension of liturgy.

Let us look at just a few of the elements of liturgy with an eye to seeing more deeply into their nature and what they require of us in order to participate fully in the ritual, the work of Christ, and the encounter with God. The four we shall examine are: the scripture readings, prayers, gestures, and time.

THE SCRIPTURE READINGS:
THE WORD OF GOD FOR THE PEOPLE OF GOD

In English we use the term "word," as opposed to "words," to refer to the message as a whole: "word got around that Paul was in trouble" or "she sat there all day, waiting for the word that never came." The latter example hints at something further. When we use the term "word" in phrases like "just say the word" or "he gave the word" or "she gave her word" or "he put in a word" or "she took him at his word," we are indicating more than the simple transfer of information. "Word" may refer to a command or a promise or some other commitment; at the very least it refers to a communication that is expected to have an effect on the receiver. "Word" often implies some degree of inter*action* between the speaker and the hearer: "he gave the word and they all jumped" or "he gave his word and they took him at his word." It implies not just saying something but doing something; and perhaps in the doing there is a disclosure, a gift, however fleeting, of one self to another. It could conceivably even take non-verbal form: the "word" given could be a prearranged signal, gesture, or symbolic gift such as a ring or plaque.

In all these ways the English term "word" begins to come close to the field of meaning within which the Hebrew term *dabar* operates. *Dabar* can mean a spoken word, but it is also widely used to refer to an event or experience of some significance. Perhaps the classic example is to be found in the Gospel of Luke, where the semiticism has survived in the Greek and is retained in the old Douay-Rheims version. After the angels have delivered the good tidings to certain shepherds in the hills near Bethlehem, the shepherds say to one another: "Let us go over to Bethlehem, and let us *see this word that is come to pass*, which the Lord hath showed to us (Luke 2:25)." It is this conception of the Word of God as event that underlies the teaching of *Dei verbum:*

> [The] deeds wrought by God in the history of salvation manifest and confirm the teaching and realities signified by the words, while the words proclaim the deeds and clarify the mystery contained in them.[5]

Thus, before it is put into words, and long before it is put into Scripture, the word of God is communicated in the form of historical events requiring interpretation. The Exodus, for example, was interpreted by the Israelites as a word of God; for the Egyptians it was something else altogether. The same has to be said of all the great events of Israel's history and even of what is sometimes referred to as "the Christ event": the person, life and death of Jesus of Nazareth. In each case, the *dabar* was an event that needed interpretation. Even the selection of the event for interpretation is itself a preliminary interpretation; not everything that happened to Israel or everything that happened to Jesus or the apostles has survived in the selective memory of the canonical tradition in the written word. We know from John's Gospel that even the writers were aware of this: "Now Jesus did many other signs in the presence of his disciples, which are not written in this book. But these are written so that you may come to believe that Jesus is the Messiah, the Son of God, and that through believing you may have life in his name" (John 20:30-31). What is written is sufficient for the faith of the Church.

We can, therefore, distinguish at least three phases of the word of God:

1. the *event* that is experienced in particular time and place but which is also seen, by some at least, as not just of purely mundane significance, but as disclosing what *Dei verbum* calls "the mystery";

2. the *interpretation of the event* that begins in the very experience of the event itself but then unfolds in celebration, narration, reflection, legislation, poetry, and so on;

3. the *written text*, or Scripture, originates as an *aide-memoire*, to keep the memory alive, but often, too, as a polemic against alternative interpretations of the same event.

Thus it is inaccurate to identify the word of God with Scriptures alone. The Bible exists now as a single, closed collection that is read by and to people who profess the God of the Bible to be their God. How does it operate as a communication of the word of God?

First, as we have seen, the Scriptures must be viewed as the literary production of a people who for centuries lived by the word of God. Another way to say this is that they lived through part of the world's history and experienced their part of it as sacramental in some sense. They read the signs of the times as indications, gestures, interventions of God, summoning them to respond. Their response took the form of interpreting and remembering, where the interpretation was a lived interpretation and the remembering was a matter of being faithful to what God had disclosed. In the Bible, "remembering" is the opposite of forgetting: the sinner forgets the ways of God, the just remember and meditate on the law as they live it; conversely, God is asked to remember the promise of the past and to forget the sins of the people. To remember is to live and act in a way that is congruent with that which is remembered.

Second, one must understand that the remembering revealed in the Scriptures constituted an ongoing engagement of the people with God both in the present and onward into the future. The God of the Exodus was the God of creation, the God of Israel now and forever. The primordial Exodus event led to a reinterpretation of the past and a new set of projections for the future. Thus, memory for Israel as for everyone became the key to making sense of all that had been, all that was, and all that might yet be. Memory makes re-membering possible, the exercise of seeking the pattern that makes experience intelligible. For Israel, the memory of the past enabled present and future to be understood in turn as part of the continuing speech of God, calling each generation into convenantal partnership with God in shaping life and history. This in turn required continuing reinterpretation by the community, understanding the present in light of the past and the past in light of present and future.

The Scriptures then can become word of God whenever they are proclaimed in the assembly gathered for the purpose of hearing that word. The word is not precisely the text as such but the communication-event that transpires when the assembly is confronted by God as a Thou through the medium of the text proclaimed. The people, hearing the ancient text in the circumstances of a particular present, know themselves addressed in that present: once again, memory renders the present intelligible and interprets it as a present moment of mutual presence. Thus the word is not in the words but in the communication; not in the mind of the author, but in the heart of the Church which knows itself to be summoned and addressed by Christ, in whom the one Word was first made flesh. "[In] the liturgy God speaks to His people and Christ is still proclaiming His Gospel."[6] The proclamation of the Scriptures is the outward, audible, and visible sign of the hidden, inaudible, invisible presence of Christ himself proclaiming the Word to the circle of his disciples.

This experience of the Word of God is to be given voice in the homily and herein lies the importance of that action in the liturgy. At its best it, too, shares with the scriptural readings the nature of a sacrament:

> The sermon . . . . should draw its content mainly from the scriptural and liturgical sources. Its character should be that of a proclamation of God's wonderful works in the history of salvation, that is, the mystery of Christ ever made present and active within us, especially in the celebration of the liturgy.[7]

The role of the homily is not to instruct or entertain; nor is the role of the homilist to pursue any agenda other than that of facilitating the spark of communication between old texts and a contemporary assembly. That spark is itself the Word of God: "Were not our hearts burning within us while he was talking to us on the road, while he was opening the scriptures to us?" (Luke 24:32). What Guardini said of the priest during the Eucharistic Prayer applies equally well to the preacher in the liturgy of the word: "It would be sacrilegious if a man pretended to speak and act on his own account in a matter which is beyond all human capacity to accomplish."[8]

The word is effective, said St. Augustine, "not because it is said, but because it is believed."[9] The voice of God will be heard speaking in the Scriptures not because Church teaching says so, but because the conditions are right for hearing with faith. In the long term, this means an adequate biblically-based catechesis that will prepare the faithful to undertake the hermeneutic required for hearing ancient texts as living word. In the more immediate context of the liturgy, it means creating the conditions that will encourage the "emptiness" of which we spoke earlier and at the same time project the exercise of reading the Scriptures in the Church as a sacramental act. The Presence of Christ in the Scriptures has to be appropriately ritualized with attention to place, objects, gestures, music, and above all the proclamation.

It is striking that the documents on the liturgy prefer to speak of "proclaiming the word" rather than of reading the Scriptures. This phraseology points to the *res et sacramentum* or reality signified by the exercise of public reading in the assembly: the reading is the lector's, the text is Paul's, but the word is Christ's. For that to become anything more than a theological conceit, however, it has to be translated into ritual action in ways analogous to those in which the presence of Christ in the Eucharist is made credible. The point of showing respect for the book, for example, is to encourage reverence for the word of God, and reverence for the word of God must lead to the obedience of faith. Ritualizing the word would fall into aestheticism or bibliolatry if it did not serve to foster an attitude of vulnerability before the word. As Karl Barth saw, being vulnerable to what the word implies a profound inner silence, in which all our preoccupations die away, in which all that we bring into God's presence falls away, in which we ourselves become hollow and receptive.

THE PRAYERS: THE WORD OF THE CHURCH

According to the prophet Isaiah, the word that proceeds from God does not return to God empty, that is, without doing God's will and accomplishing all that it was sent to do (Isa 55:10-11). The word that proceeds from the eternal silence of God and makes its home in our silence rises back to God enfleshed in the prayer of the Church. The prayer of the Church is the prayer of Christ the Word, wrought in us by the Spirit who prays in a way that is too deep for words (Rom 8:26). What does that mean?

In her *Last Tales*, Isak Dinesen speaks of various levels of storytelling, the deepest of which is the story that cannot be told, the story of who we really are.[10] This is the story we try to piece together for ourselves on the basis of the fragmentary stories we can tell. If I wanted to tell you what my mother is like, the kind of person she is, I would not give you her curriculum vitae. That would only tell you what happened to her and what she did in her life. To tell you what she is like, I would have to tell you stories about her. From the stories you will guess the story that cannot be told.

So also with God. The story of God is a story that can never be told. We tell stories of God, but the ultimate story of God is beyond our telling and, if truth be told, beyond our imagining. That is why the Bible has so many stories. That is why we have four Gospels instead of a definitive official biography of Jesus. It is all to point beyond the stories that can be told to the story that cannot be told.

So also with the prayer of the Church. The prayers of the Church must never be taken literally, as if they exhausted all that there was to be said. They are at best stammerings, shots in the dark, utterly inadequate attempts to give voice to a prayer that is beyond all words. That prayer beyond all words is the prayer of the Son, and the name of that prayer is Spirit. The Spirit is the name we give to the yearning of the Son for the Father and of the Father for the Son, the eternal delight of the Son in the Father and the Father in the Son, the utterly unfathomable devotion of the Father for the Son and of the Son for the Father. Since that same Spirit in the sheer exuberance of divine love has been poured out upon human beings, we too have been caught up in the love of the Father and the Son, and in the eternal prayer of the Son to the Father. That prayer is the prayer beyond telling. It takes the form of words and stories, but it is not the words, it is not the stories. It is rather the yearning of the Spirit, making the Word into flesh, making the flesh of history into Word. For what comes to us as Word returns to God as prayer.

More prosaically, the words used in the liturgy represent speech-acts of various kinds; to regard them as bits of information transmitted to God would be a profound misunderstanding. While not devoid of semantic content, they are first and foremost utterances that involve and commit the participants in relation to one another, to Christ and to God.

There are utterances exchanged within the assembly itself, as when the priest and people greet each other, or when the baptizer says solemnly, "N., I baptize you in the name of the Father and of the Son and of the Holy Spirit," or when the assembly acknowledges the faith of the parents and godparents by singing: "This is our faith. This is the faith we are proud to profess in Christ Jesus our Lord." Many texts, including admonitions, invitations, exhortations, and blessings, fall into this category.

There are prayers addressed to God the Father through Christ. This is in fact the norm for liturgical prayer, as laid down by the Council of Carthage in 397: that prayer at the altar is always to be addressed to the Father through the Son in the Holy Spirit. Eucharistic prayers almost invariably follow this form as do the collects and other presidential prayers. There are also congregational acclamations, usually addressed to Christ, as in the *Kyrie* and the *Agnus Dei*, but also some addressed to God, such as the first part of the *Gloria* and the *Sanctus*.

Unfortunately, this pattern of prayer, i.e., addressed to the Father, is often obscured in local assemblies. The intercessions, for example, are sometimes addressed to Christ or the assembly itself or even to no one in particular ("May all who have died be granted eternal rest"). For this reason it is important to examine the nature of prayer in some key texts of the liturgy—the psalms, the collects and the eucharistic prayer—as cases in point.

In the early centuries of the Church and on through the Middle Ages, the psalter was the prayer book not only of the monks and clergy, but of all who were both devout and literate. The coupling of these conditions is not arbitrary, for the psalter was the first reader for children at least up until the Reformation. More importantly, it served to initiate generation after generation into the art of Christian prayer, being presented to the candidates for baptism in some churches but serving as a model of prayer for all. This was made possible both through a judicious selection of psalms (it was only a monastic practice to read them all through in order) and through the practice of "christianizing" them. Though the latter procedure has come in for heavy criticism in modern times, it was the immediate expression of a deeply Christian instinct for seeing all things "in Christ."

The net effect was to train individuals to pray in the name of another and to subordinate their own immediate needs and gratifications to the larger hopes and joys of redeemed humanity. Only in such a frame of mind could praying the psalter make sense, with requests such as for God to "subdue peoples under our feet" (Ps 47), with descriptions such as "by the rivers of Bablyon—there we sat down and there we wept when we remembered Zion" (Ps 137), and even such cries as "My soul longs, indeed it faints for the courts of the Lord" (Ps 84). If prayer was meant to be the outpouring of individual hearts, how could verses like these ever be appointed for collective use?

Psalm prayer, therefore, represents a certain discipline of mind and heart, requiring those who pray the psalms to enter into and identify with the joys and hopes, the griefs and anxieties of the whole human race. It is possible to begin doing this simply by praying the psalms as the prayer of Christ, as if it were his voice praying through us. By doing so we can participate in his submission to God in life and in death, as well as his experience of deliverance out of death that constitutes the fundamental pattern in which the baptized not merely imitate but share. This was possible because in becoming human, the Son of God had taken upon himself and redeemed all the joys and sufferings of humanity. In turn, this identification of Christ with every last human being seemed to require the same identification on the part of those who would identify with him. If Christ had shared our human condition so that we might share his divine condition, it could only be by identifying with the human condition that we could hope to share his divine life. In short, the prayer of the psalms that voices so movingly the whole range of human emotions, was prayed as the prayer of Christ and in Christ as the prayer of the whole human race throughout every phase of the paschal mystery and in very epoch of human history.

In considering the collects, we see that being able to pray them presupposes the sort of training provided by the psalter, for they are equally alien. They pray for graces of rather abstract kind: "show us the way to peace in this world"; "protect the good you have given us"; "may we live the faith we profess and trust your promise of eternal life." Attempts to provide more concrete and substantial petitions in the alternative opening prayers have not always been successful. The difficulty seems to lie not only in the telegrammatic form of the collect genre, but with the requirement that a prayer to be used always and everywhere speak to (or out of) the here and now.

While the effort to develop a genuinely English form of opening prayer to replace the highly condensed Latin collect is well worth pursuing, the fact of the matter is that the prayer of the liturgy is never going to be perfectly expressive of any particular assembly, except by accident. It will never be specifically relevant because it is always the prayer of the larger Church. If it is made relevant, by the presider praying spontaneously for example, something will be gained, but something equally will certainly be lost. What will be lost is what is produced by the very fact that the prayer itself says (i.e., communicates to us) little or nothing about ourselves. At best, it speaks of the world we know only in the most general terms and holds before us vague promises and undefined hopes with regard to an indeterminate future. Perhaps we could do better with improvised prayer, but to the degree that the prayer is immediate and concrete and specific to this time and place, the prayer will lose its objectivity. The loss of objectivity, in turn, is likely to blind us to the most important fact about the collect: it is not our prayer at all!

Like all the solemn prayers of the liturgy offered by the presider in the name of the Church, the collect is a faint and distorted echo of the prayer of Christ before the throne of God. That is why it is always to be addressed to God, never to the Son or the Holy Spirit. It is addressed to the Father, as Hippolytus said in the third century, *through* the Son, *in* the Holy Spirit *in the holy Church*. The point of the exercise every time a collect is offered is for the gathered Church to attune itself, as it were, to the prayer of Christ arising from the depths of the Spirit. The call to prayer and the brief moment of silence that precede it are a precious opportunity for members of the community to lower themselves gently into those depths of the Spirit. It is not a time for thinking what we would like to pray for or for formulating our own intentions. It is a time for immersion in collective silence so that behind the words articulated by the presider, the *prayer* without words may be overheard arising before the throne of God.

Lastly, we consider the Eucharistic Prayer. Perhaps more than anywhere else, we see in the Eucharistic Prayer (whichever anaphora is used) that what the Church says to God is at the same time a word/*dabar* of God. Prayer is at once humanity's response to God and at the very same time God's own word and act in us.

On the face of it, a Eucharistic Prayer is a faith narrative, a confession or acknowledgement of God. It is a remembering of the story of God, a story glimpsed in the episodes recalled from creation to the end of time. The past, only ever recalled in fragments, such as an episode or two from the history of Israel or the life of Jesus, is not over and done with. It continues to work itself out now and into the future ordained by God, a future already partially realized in the present. The anamnesis is the remembering of a story that cannot be told but only alluded to: "Christ has died, Christ is risen, Christ will come again." It is a story told as the story we and all humanity are living in.

This is not then just the story of God. Because we are living in it, it is our story also. Best of all we could say that it is a common story: the story of God and us, the story of God's appeal to human freedom. Its most important moment is not the institution narrative, the recalling of the mandate that grounds this celebration, but the epiclesis or invocation of the Holy Spirit. The epiclesis is the Church's prayer for the continuing gift of the Spirit that is in Christ Jesus. It is a prayer that the story we are living *in* may also be the story we are living *out*: that the story of God and the story of our lives may become one story. Especially in the Eucharist this story is told as a story of communion:

> May all of us who share in the body and blood of Christ be brought together in unity by the Holy Spirit (Eucharistic Prayer II).

> Grant that we, who are nourished by his body and blood,
> may be filled with his Holy Spirit,
> and become one body, one spirit in Christ (Eucharistic Prayer III).

> By your Holy Spirit,
> gather all who share this one bread and one cup,
> into the one body of Christ, a living sacrifice of praise (Eucharistic Prayer IV).

By anamnesis and epiclesis, by the words that accompany the action of eating and drinking together, the convention of eating and drinking becomes the sign and the realization of God's action in our action. It is the spoken word of the Church that indicates the *res tantum*, the ultimate meaning of the gesture: the assembly, united around the one bread and the one cup, becomes a *dabar* of God, the latest realization of God's unutterable Word.

In the Eucharist and all the sacraments the form of the sacrament is a word of God in the words of the Church: the very response of the Church by which the Church submits to God and conjoins its activity with God's activity, becomes both the Word-act of Christ mediating God's grace to us and the prayer of Christ for us to God. We are sanctified, the Body is built up, and God is glorified: these are three effects of the saving Word that is also *prayer*.

If the words of the prayers are merely echoes at best of the unspoken *prayer* between Christ and the Father, then it is essential not to rattle off the words as if we were leaving a message on someone's answering machine. Rather, the prayer recited must echo the silence, hinting in its mode of recitation at the movement of the Spirit out of and back into the stillness of God. This means again that we need a context of deep silence.

"The word must die," Paul Ricoeur once wrote, "to serve that which was spoken."[11] The biblical word, like the word of prayer, arises out of silence and dies away into silence: only "that which was spoken" abides. We are all too often drowned in words, and silences are awkward, restless intermissions in a constant stream of verbal and kinetic bombardment. For our liturgy to "work," for the prayer to become the prayer of Christ, for the readings to be heard as word of God, it all needs to float on a sea of silence. Such silence is not the absence of noise; it is the depth dimension of all that is said and seen and done. It has to be restored as the depth dimension of the acclamations and chants of the liturgy, as well as the movements and gestures of the rite. It is to that aspect of the liturgy that we now turn our attention.

GESTURES OF THE LITURGY: EMBODIED PRAYER FORMS

Once again, it is Romano Guardini who leads us directly to the heart of the matter:

> [T]hose whose task it is to teach and educate will have to ask themselves—and this is all-decisive—whether they themselves desire the liturgical act or, to put it plainly, whether they know of its existence and what exactly it consists of and that it is neither a luxury nor an oddity, but a matter of fundamental importance. Or does it, basically, mean the same to them as to the parish priest of the late nineteenth century who said: "We must organize the procession better; we must see to it that the singing and the praying is done better." He did not realize that he should have asked himself quite a different question: how can the act of walking become a religious act, a retinue for the Lord progressing through his land, so that an "epiphany" may take place.[12]

Notice that Guardini is not advocating that we explain the gestures to people but that we learn to do them in such a way that, in the words of the liturgy constitution, the visible is subordinated and directed to the invisible, the human to the divine, action to contemplation. Edward Fischer made a similar plea to educators in his book, *Everybody Steals from God*:

> Religious educators need to work harder at communicating the idea that the *way* something is done is at the very foundation of the religious life. No activity is religious if it lowers life, and none is secular once it lifts life. *How* a thing is done is rock-bottom communication that goes beyond all words and turns an act into one of worship or into a blasphemy.[13]

In thinking of how the gestures of the rite might become epiphanies, it is tempting to focus on the great gestures of the liturgy like baptismal immersion, the breaking of bread or the act of anointing with chrism. But if the whole liturgy is in principle an act of Christ, an exercise in visible form of his invisible, heavenly mediation, then we ought to be able to undertake the same exploration in regard to the humbler gestures of the rite, such as walking, standing, genuflecting, or kneeling. How do these become epiphanies? Such a question is not addressed only to liturgy planners, but to every worshipper in the assembly.

Rituals are symbols in action, and the meaning of ritual is directly available only in the enactment and only to those who enact them. Ritual is not intended to communicate its meaning to spectators but to participants. Consequently, the principles that follow are above all principles governing the enactment of ritual and are verified (or falsified) in the *doing*. This is true even when the actual gesture is performed only by one of the participants, e.g., the presider. All others are co-participants, identifying with the action by their presence and by associating themselves at least imaginatively with what is being done.

The following are principles that govern ritual behavior and may help us to participate more fully in the liturgical gestures. First of all, gestures are symbolic. The liturgy uses visible signs to signify invisible things. In other words, while there may be some things that happen at liturgy that are purely functional—as when someone gets up and opens a window—*all that belongs to the rite is symbolic*. In fact, one of the basic skills required of participants is that of being able to distinguish what belongs to the rite from what is extraneous (e.g., the presider blowing his nose is extraneous, but what about when he washes his hands? What about the assembly sitting for the readings?). All that belongs to the rite is in some way or other significant: the sprinkling with water, the procession to Communion, the sitting, standing and kneeling of the assembly, even the taking up of the collection.

These are symbolic actions; there is more going on here than meets the eye. The empirical movement or posture is the bearer of symbolic meaning, first for the agent, then for the assembly as a whole. Drinking from the chalice is not the same as drinking a cup of water at the sink; standing for the gospel is not the same as standing to stretch or even standing to sing; sitting for the readings is not the same as sitting to rest your legs; standing in line for Communion is not the same as standing in line at a checkout counter or even the same as standing in line to have your throat blessed on the feast of St. Blaise. The difference may be hard to pinpoint—like the difference between a wink and a nervous twitch or a grimace and a smile. It is a difference that lies less in the act itself than in the understanding that when the act is done in the liturgical context it becomes a symbolic action. Knowledge of the code tells those familiar with the symbol system that something non-pragmatic is transpiring. One belongs to a cultural code, the other does not. One promises to make sense, the other does not. Gesture is a form of language; more than just a movement, it is a way of saying something.

Ritual gestures are redundant, that is, there is something excessive (or minimalistic) about them. The "unnecessary" aspects signal that something non-pragmatic is going on, suggesting the difference between eating and dining, between walking and processing, between passing an object to another person and presenting it to him or her. When the Queen of England opens Parliament, she does not stomp in, head straight for her throne, slump back, and take the weight off her legs. The act of walking is more than a way of getting from the coach to the throne: it is an epiphany of majesty. And the act of sitting is more than resting: it is the assumption of rule and the manifestation of authority. Majesty, rule, and authority are intangibles that take on visible form when ordinary things are done in a particular way.

In the liturgy, as elsewhere in life, actions become deliberate, movements stylized, relationships formalized. Food and drink become more—or less—than mere hunger or thirst would require. Dress, far from being functional, often becomes quite dysfunctional: a crown will scarcely protect the head from the weather, a presider does not wear three to four layers of clothing for warmth. The shortest distance from the sacristy to the altar will be taken by the sacristan, but the ministers will take the long way round to open the liturgy. Sometimes, however, the gesture is identifiably symbolic because it is less than would otherwise be necessary: as when the mayor digs the first shovel full for the construction of a new town hall, or when baptism is less than a bath and the bread and wine of the Eucharist less than a banquet. Such departure from the norm says that the activity in question is symbolic, that food and clothing and gesture have ceded their pragmatic role in human life to assume a signifying function.

This formal quality of ritual behavior presents something of a problem for many people today. Doesn't ritual behavior inhibit authentic behavior? Doesn't it breed insincerity? How can I be myself if I have to put on an act?

The assumption underlying these objections seems to be that the only authentic gestures are those that express how we feel. Truthfulness, it seems to be suggested, can only be observed in a spontaneous expression of emotion or in a personally formulated reporting of one's inner thoughts, beliefs, and sentiments: like leaping into the air on winning the lottery or bursting into tears when one is distraught. Getting in touch with one's real feelings is obviously a worthwhile objective, and the ability to acknowledge and express one's feelings is clearly desirable. There are occasions when such expressions are appropriate and many more occasions when they are not.

The problem with liturgy is that while it may on occasion be cathartic, it does not set out to be so. For one thing, there is simply no way of guaranteeing that everyone is going to feel the same way on any given occasion or at any given point in the liturgy. More importantly, there is something more basic at work in the context of liturgy than feeling, and that is *attitude.*

Often it is hard to distinguish attitudes and feelings, especially since feelings are not infrequently tied to basic attitudes. But it is finally our attitudes that make us who we are. Our attitudes represent the way our lives are pointed, the more or less habitual ways of thinking, feeling, and acting that shape and color our lives and make us the persons we are. What is your attitude toward capital punishment, or abortion, or sports, or your work? How do you feel about gay rights, or South Africa, or affirmative action, or the present pope? Feelings in this sense represent our attitudes, and our attitudes represent our commitments. Such commitments may on occasion require that we overrule our feelings of reluctance or revulsion or apathy or whatever and act in accordance with the attitudes we wish to make our own. Visiting a dying friend may not be what we feel like doing, but we go anyway. Participating in a conversation with someone we always find slightly irritating may be something prompted by conscience rather than feeling. Similarly with liturgy. If we only went to church when we felt like it, we would probably cease feeling like it rather soon. If we only knelt when everyone in the assembly felt humble, kneeling would never happen. If only those who felt connected to the rest of the assembly could exchange a gesture of peace, we would have a very different experience of the communion rite.

But liturgy is not an expression of emotions; it is a rehearsal of attitudes. Kneeling to confess one's sin may not be what one would spontaneously feel like doing on a sunny spring morning, but the liturgy tells us that in the presence of God an attitude of humility and self-abasement is appropriate. We may not feel like standing alert and still at the proclamation of the gospel, but it is what the liturgy calls us to do. On occasion, perhaps at a funeral, Mass of Thanksgiving, or Easter Vespers, the liturgy may strike just the right note and everything—heart and mind and emotions—will come together in a way that really carries us away. But for most people, that is a relatively rare experience. Liturgy will not leave us on an emotional high because that is not its purpose. But regular, persevering participation and growing familiarity with liturgy's images and gestures will eventually shape our attitudes, our thoughts, and even our feelings. To expect the liturgy to echo our feelings is to court disappointment; to try to shape the liturgy to manipulate people's feelings is to court disaster. The liturgy is there for us to enter into: "O come in, let us worship and bow down, let us kneel before the Lord our maker. . . ." (Ps 95:6).

According to Jonathan Z. Smith, ritual is a way of attending to something.[14] Allowing the ritual to guide our attention, we will find ourselves anew in the breaking of bread, in the beating of the breast, in the bowing and bending, in the gesture of peace. Liturgy is ritual: not improvisation but discipline, not spontaneity but practice. It is the rehearsal of a role we shall take a lifetime to grow into. It is our sanctification.

God is glorified when we make room for God's presence and allow God's action to find its full scope in our lives. It is the John the Baptist principle: we must decrease so that Christ may increase. We must be de-centered, so that Christ may stand at the center of our existence. When allowed to be itself, liturgy will do just that. Through the prayer and gestures of the liturgy, we open ourselves up to the prayer of the Spirit praying in us. Through conforming to the constraints of the rite, we de-center ourselves, momentarily abandon our claim to autonomy, so that our bodies might become epiphanies of Christ in our midst.

TIME: THE CONTEXT OF THE LITURGY

Of all the languages of the rite, perhaps the most neglected or underrated is time. The liturgy constitution speaks of the Church as in this present world, yet in it as a sign of the world to come. Especially in the liturgical assembly, this ambivalence of the Church colors the whole proceedings, for it is here that what T.S. Eliot called "the intersection of the timeless with time" transpires.[15] It is nothing less than the irruption of the eschatological *future* into the *present* on the basis of the *past*.

The timing of the liturgy, therefore, has always been a matter of some importance. The assembly of the faithful quickly became established on the first day of the week, not because Sunday is intrinsically holy, but because that day had associations for Christians—as the first day of creation, the day of resurrection, the first day of the new creation—and opting to gather regularly on that day, rather than say the Sabbath, said something about who they were and what the Eucharist was. A quite different set of meanings would have been engendered if like the Rotary Club they had decided to meet for lunch every other Monday, or if they had decided to meet on Thursday nights because that was when the Last Supper had been held. Similarly with the decision to break with the Jewish Passover as the anniversary of the Christian Pasch and to celebrate it every year on a Sunday instead. Similarly with the feast of Christmas in the fourth century: the date is not, of course, the date of Christ's birth, but the selection of December 25 (however that might have been arrived at) was part of the language of the rite. It was significant. What its original significance was is now uncertain. Was it the Christians' response to the pagan midwinter festivities in Rome? Or rather was it arrived at by working forward from the conception of Christ on March 25? The association of March 25 with the death of Christ means that Christmas once trailed associations with Easter, now long since lost. But in the northern hemisphere, the celebration of the birth of Christ in the depths of winter darkness has accumulated associations over the centuries that are problematic for Christians of the (relatively) newly populated southern hemisphere.

Out of these developments grew a calendar, and out of the calendar grew a rhythm of feast and fast, of holy days and holy seasons, the passage of the year marked by the colors of the vestments, the chants of the *Introits*, the endless carousel of saints, the recurrence of hot cross buns and Easter eggs. And there was the rhythm of the day: regular prayer at meal times, the sounds of the *Angelus* bell wafting across the fields, the call to Vespers, Compline by candlelight. It is easy to romanticize and idealize the centuries of Christendom. Even non-believers have felt the pull of them.

This rhythm is long lost. In the United Sates it was never really known unless in a few utopian settlements or in the few contemplative communities that exist in this country. It seems that the Church's calendar, once the rhythm to which whole peoples moved in synch, is increasingly peripheral even to its most devout membership. Indeed, our lives are much more likely to receive their shape from the calendar of secular celebrations, running from Labor Day in September to Halloween and Thanksgiving, from Christmas to New Year's Day and Superbowl Sunday, from Valentine's Day to St. Patrick's Day and Easter, from Mother's Day to Memorial Day and the Fourth of July, and then back to Labor Day.

Part of the problem we face is that it is hard for many to distinguish between this calendar and that of the Church. Both keep Christmas and Easter and Sts. Valentine and Patrick, and churches usually find at least some way of marking Memorial Day and Thanksgiving. But the civil feasts of Christmas and Easter have little to do with the religious festivals of the same name: they do not celebrate the Incarnation or salvation or give thanks for redemption.

Moreover, in the civil calendar feasts are celebrated in the period leading up to the official date. In stores and schools and private homes, Christmas season runs from Halloween to Christmas Day; in church this is Advent, and Christmas begins on the evening of December 24 and runs until Epiphany (approximately). Similarly with Easter: it is preceded by the six weeks of Lent and celebrated by the seven weeks of Eastertide (Pentecost). The Church prepares for its feasts in sobriety and recollection; the secular world prepares for its feasts by consumption and festivity.

Such developments create quandaries for Christians. On the one hand, calendars are important clues to social identity: there are sports calendars, business calendars, financial calendars, arts calendars, and school calendars, giving shape to the sports world, the business world, the financial world, the arts world, and the educational world. Our own personal calendars represent an overlap of several of these social calendars, reflecting the various communities with which we are associated. What better indicator of the reality of pluralism?

Unfortunately, the parish seems almost entirely oblivious to this problem. When there is a clash of calendars, all too seldom is the question of meaning raised. Instead, the clash is resolved in terms of convenience. It is convenience that determines the number and times of Masses. It is convenience that dictates that the Easter Vigil must be abbreviated to fit into the time slot between supper and bedtime (whereas a vigil, by definition, means the disruption of our usual schedules of eating and sleeping). It is convenience that decides that the school schedule should have priority over the liturgical calendar so we will have Christmas parties in Advent, the spring dance on the fifth Friday of Lent, and First Communions at the end of the spring semester instead of during Easter because everyone is on break then.

The calendar creates the rhythm, the rhythm creates the dance, the dance creates communion—with the community of faith, with the cosmos, with God.

Part of our liturgical renewal must take the form of being attentive to the mysteries revealed in the rhythmic language of time. The point about the observance of the holy days, about the rhythm of the day and week and seasons, is that it is a primary form of liturgical participation, engrafting us into a larger scheme of things, enabling us to find our place in the world and move in step with the rhythm of the universe. The here and now are redeemed from meaninglessness by being connected to the always and everywhere. We are relieved of the burden of giving meaning to what we do by finding a cosmic context in which our little joys and pains are part of a larger mystery, the "liturgy of the world." It is this that Morning and Evening Hours do, this that Midday Prayer and Compline do. Every dawn is a new dawn, a new beginning, a new age, a new creation, a resurrection; every evening is the evening of the world, a fading of the light, the end of history, the perennial passage from light to darkness, from motion to stillness, from sounds to silence, the rehearsal of the sleep of death.

Liturgy has two dimensions, the canonical and the indexical.[16] The canonical dimension is that which is unchanging and which represents thereby the permanence of the Always and Everywhere. The indexical dimension consists of all the traces of the particular, of the here and now. The art is to allow the intersection of history and now, of everywhere and this place, of this time and this hour, now with eternity; of these people—this man, this woman, given in marriage, lately deceased, new-born, penitent, sick, anointed, welcomed—with the people of all ages, with the God of ages. Too much of the canonical and the liturgy will be rigid, distant, unconnected, awesome but ultimately irrelevant. Too much of the indexical, too much of the here and now, and the liturgy deflates into a celebration of who we are, cut off from those who have gone before us and those who will come after us, cut loose from our moorings in eternity, drifting like a ship of fools on a sea of meaninglessness, living for the now because we know of nothing else.

That is why the objectivity of the liturgy must be respected, with its holy texts, its holy words, its holy gestures, its holy objects, and its holy rhythms, so that we, as named individuals, with named needs, at this particular time and place, at this particular juncture in history, at this particular moment in our lives, in our week, in our day, can be plugged in to the greater whole. Plugged in, engrafted, inserted, rooted; and then assumed, taken up, transformed by the rites into that which runs from alpha to omega, from the beginning to the end of time and beyond.

More prosaically, symbols (which are our connectors) depend on memory, on pattern and repetition that engender recognition and even anticipation. Through the familiarity bred of consistency and repetition, the mystery begins to glow, like the genie's lamp that worked only when it was rubbed. But we suffer from the practical heresy of believing that insight comes only with the new and unfamiliar, that repetition breeds only boredom, and that the old is old hat and must be discarded. This is a practical heresy as dangerous as any theological heresy, for it cuts us off from the sources of life in the liturgical practices of the Church. Time is one of the languages of the liturgy. It is only at our peril that we manage it according to the canons of convenience. For better or for worse, we are shaped by the way we spend our time.

CONCLUSION

This chapter has presented a contemplative approach to selected aspects of the liturgy, attempting to explicate what Guardini hinted at when he spoke of the "liturgical act" and of "lost attitudes" and "a forgotten way of doing things." The "liturgical act" is essentially a sacramental mindset, a way of looking and seeing more than meets the eye. It has everything to do with faith, "the assurance of things hoped for, the conviction of things not seen" (Heb 11:1), brought to bear on any part of the liturgy or on the liturgy as a whole. It is ultimately an encounter with, in, and through liturgy for the sake of the world.

Notes

1. "A Letter from Romano Guardini," in *Herder Correspondence* (August 1964) 237.

2. Ibid.

3. *The Varieties of Religious Experience* (New York: Vintage Books, 1990) 36.

4. *Herder Correspondence*, 237–38.

5. DV 2.

6. SC 33. See also SC 7: "[Christ] is present in His word, since it is He Himself who speaks when the holy Scriptures are read in the church."

7. SC 35(2).

8. *Liturgie und liturgische Bildung* (Wuerzburg: Werkbund, 1966) 190.

9. Tractate 80, *On John* 15.1-3, *The Fathers of the Church: St. Augustine Tractates on the Gospel of John*, trans. John W. Rittig (Washington, D.C.: The Catholic University of American Press, 1994) 117.

10. *Last Tales* (New York: Random House, 1957).

11. The editors have been unable to locate the source of this quote but saw it as important to the development of the text.

12. *Herder Correspondence*, 238.

13. *Everybody Steals from God* (Notre Dame, Ind.: University of Notre Dame Press, 1977) 124 (emphasis original).

14. *To Take Place: Toward Theory in Ritual* (Chicago: University of Chicago Press, 1987) 103ff.

15. "The Dry Salvages," *The Complete Poems and Plays 1909–1950* (New York: Harcourt, Brace & World, 1971) 136.

16. Rappaport, "The Obvious Aspects of Ritual," 179ff.

4 The Outward/ Public Dimension of Liturgy

The premise of this work is that it is possible to develop a fuller, more conscious, and more active participation by moving in two directions at once: toward a more contemplative approach *and* toward greater social awareness. We need to develop the inwardness of our liturgy, as well as its outwardness. Both are important. If we develop only the inward and contemplative dimension of liturgy, with which we have been concerned in previous chapters, there is the danger of not fully sounding its depths, in which case we may simply end up with an introverted, privatized style of liturgy. On the other hand, we have a healthy tradition of social activism in the Church that sometimes seems to offer an alternative to the contemplative tradition and to liturgy. But if we let that alone shape our approach to liturgy, we run the risk of turning it into a platform for social and political issues, accentuating the verbal and communitarian aspects of the rite, and perhaps minimizing the more formal and deeper dimensions of the rituals that belong to the rite. In order to move toward a new synthesis of inward and outward participation, we need to explore the inherently social character of the liturgy itself.

TOWARD PUBLIC WORSHIP

Thanks to the tireless work of Virgil Michel and others, one of the distinctive features of the liturgical movement in North America was precisely the forging of the connection between the liturgy itself and the forms of social life. This connection is based on our common baptism, which makes us all members of the one organic Body of Christ. Baptism was seen by the liturgical pioneers not as the sacrament which saved individual souls, but as the incorporation of the individual into a collectivity in which the uniqueness of the person is respected, while the essentially social dimension of the personality is also recognized. The Church, and especially its liturgy, bridges the gap between our private lives and our public selves in a way that has few parallels. For Virgil Michel, the Mystical Body, of which we are all members by virtue of our baptism, is a "harmonious combination of the two complementary factors of humankind, that is, organic fellowship coupled with full respect for human personality and individual responsibility."[1]

This is not just an abstract truth but a reality that is basic to our Christian lives, whether we know it or not. The God of our private prayer is the God of our public worship, indeed, God of all the earth. Through baptism, we have been made sharers in the one life of God, so we are members of one another, and the Spirit we have in common is far more basic than the particularities that differentiate us. It is this fundamental fact of life that is rehearsed over and over again in the liturgy. As Virgil Michel put it:

> [The liturgy] always puts the idea of fellowship in Christ into full practice. . . . [It] not only teaches us what this [true Christian] spirit is but also has us *live* this spirit in all its enactments.[2]

For Virgil Michel the essential continuity between liturgy and the social order had both a negative and a positive side. Positively, the liturgy rehearses and embodies the spirit of solidarity, of self-sacrifice for the common good, and proper use of the material goods of creation. On the negative side, liturgy and social justice are related because they both suffer from the same common enemies—radical individualism (freedom without commitment) and totalitarian socialism (commitment without freedom). Hence Michel's dictum:

> If the first purpose of the liturgical movement is to lead the faithful into more intimate participation in the liturgy of the Church, then the further objective must also be of getting the liturgical spirit to radiate forth from the altar of Christ into every aspect of the daily life of the Christian.[3]

For this reason, Virgil Michel saw liturgical renewal as the key to ecclesial renewal. If people could only begin to draw their spiritual sustenance from the common prayer of the Church instead of from their private devotions, he thought, this could only result in the creation of "a healthy social atmosphere" of ongoing community commitment to the corporal and spiritual works of mercy:

> For in the parish there is no distinction of persons, neither of race nor of color. Before the altar of God, all distinctions of class and race are abolished: all are equal at the communion rail and in the confessional. The same must be true of *all* parish activities and of the entire Christian life, whose inspiration must always come from the altar of Christ.[4]

These were bold and challenging words in the America of the 1930s. What are their implications for today? I would want to pose the challenge as follows: we have moved from *private* Mass (celebrated in public) to *community* celebrations, but how do we get from there to *public* worship? In other words, the pre-Vatican II Eucharist was usually celebrated for private intentions; the post-Vatican II Eucharist has tended to be celebrated for our shared intentions. But how can we learn to celebrate the Eucharist for public intentions?

TOWARD A PUBLIC CHURCH

A major obstacle to a recovery of public worship (the full implications of that term will be spelled out shortly) lies in an image of Church that lingers in our subconscious. Vatican II broke with the centuries-old image of the Church as the unique ark of salvation and with the supposition that the Church ought to be co-terminus with the human race. This model led to the assumption that everyone had to become baptized members of the Church if they were to have any hope of being saved because, according to Cyprian's ancient axiom, "outside the Church there is no salvation." Under this model, the need for grace mediated by the sacraments of the Church was absolute, which led to the practice of baptizing first and asking questions later.

Perhaps the most important and decisive achievement of Vatican II was its coming to terms with the fact that the Roman Catholic Church had never come close to bringing the whole of humanity within its embrace and, on the face of it, never will. The idea that God only saved baptized Catholics must therefore be a misunderstanding of God's will for humankind and thus a misunderstanding of the role of the Church. In short, Vatican II taught that salvation can indeed be found outside the Church.[5]

While Catholics largely take this for granted now, the full implications for the life of the Church and for its sacramental practice have still to be realized. If the Church is not an indispensable means for the salvation of every last human soul, in the sense that not every human being seems to be called by God to be a member of the Catholic

Church, then what *is* the purpose of the Church? What exactly is the calling of those who are called to baptism? It used to be assumed that we were baptized in order to be saved, but it can no longer be assumed that this is the whole answer.

A fuller answer is suggested by the conciliar image of the Church as sacrament:

> By her relationship with Christ, the Church is a kind of sacrament or sign of intimate union with God, and of the unity of all mankind. She is also an instrument for the achievement of such union and unity.[6]

The Church is thus an efficacious sign or sacrament of intimacy with God and of unity among the peoples of the world. Its *public* responsibility is not that of enabling individuals to negotiate their way into heaven (though the salvation of the world remains its goal) but that of being a public sign that our longing for communion with one another and with God is not in vain. It has to operate, then, not only in the private realm of people's interior lives, but in the public realm where the common weal is at stake. Conversely, as members of the Church, it is the vocation of the baptized not merely to save their own souls, but to contribute to the whole work of reconciliation, public and private.

Both dimensions of unity or reconciliation—the human and the divine—need to be retained, as well as the double function to *signify* and to *bring about*. While the process of reconciliation (in the divine dimension and in the human dimension) takes many forms in the overall life of the Church, it is above all in the celebration of the Church's liturgy that this process is most explicitly signified in both dimensions and most explicitly realized, for in the liturgical assembly we have a coming together of the people that unites them simultaneously with God and with one another. The liturgy is therefore the primary locus in which the Church becomes visible as a sign: the liturgy signifies what it effects and effects what it signifies. In talking about the social dimensions of the liturgy as *public* worship then, it is important to begin with the assembly itself.

THE ASSEMBLY

As "a Company of Strangers"

"Community" is one of the words that came into prominence in post-conciliar Catholicism, and its popularity is probably due in part to its ambivalence. On the one hand, it can be used of people who have something in common, even if it be nothing more than shared geographical proximity. Thus, suburbs are sometimes spoken of as "dormitory communities." Sometimes the commonality is ethnic or racial, e.g., the Hispanic community. Sometimes, people finding themselves more or less accidentally under the same roof are spoken of as a community, e.g., a retirement community. But especially in the last case, this usage often feels unsatisfactory. Thus, we find ourselves talking about "*real* community"; but what is *real* community and how do we find it or create it? Such questions, commonly heard, betray the values and expectations attached to the term "community." "Community" is less a description of reality than it is an ideal against which the shortcomings of our common life can be measured. "There's not much sense of community at St. Adalbert's." "We need some things that will help to build community." "I miss the community we used to have at Holy Cross." "Community," it appears, is above all a feeling: a sense of belonging, of being at home, of knowing and being known. "Community" is a place where no one feels like a stranger.

I suspect that the lure of community, the secret of its appeal, lies in the fact that the experience of community-feeling is so elusive. "Community" is heavy with nostalgia for older, simpler, more settled times. There is a real danger that Westerners feel envious of the sense of community lost to us, but which is still a vital experience of peoples like the Amish, who have managed to retain their traditional ways of life intact into modern times. They are people among whom it is still possible to be born and raised, grow up and marry and have children among their own kind, and to grow old and die in the care of their own kin instead of being exposed to the loneliness and impersonality of modern life. But of course in indulging such nostalgia, we overlook the price to be paid: the lack of personal freedom, the lack of privacy, the lack of opportunity for personal advancement, the lack of progress. We, in contrast, enjoy freedoms we would be reluctant to surrender: geographical and social mobility, personal and economic independence, freedom from all kinds of petty social constraints. So there is loss and gain. Wherever we live in the Western world, we are children of the metropolis to one extent or another, and ours is a metropolitan culture. Our vast anonymous conurbations give us the opportunity to work, travel, meet people, protect our privacy, and be autonomous. But the price is loneliness; we are overcrowded and yet alone as never before. For all the real interdependence that structures our lives and makes them possible, we like to think of ourselves as independent, but the price of such independence is the cutting of the very personal ties that constitute traditional societies. In short, we can no longer go back to the village, however much we may romanticize it.

What Robert Bellah, in his landmark study of American culture, pointed to as a cult of intimacy is one response to this situation; the moving back and forth between what he called "lifestyle enclaves" is another.[7] Very often, our liturgies are used in awkward attempts to create pseudo-communities. The presider tells the assembly to turn and introduce themselves to one another; the preacher speaks of the parish as a "family"; hands are held at the Our Father. But all this seems to be playing make-believe community, pretending to be a community that can never be. It can ultimately be alienating, for it invites all the participants to see reality other than it actually is. The parish is not a village clustered around its village church, where the church is the only game in town. The medieval village was long ago left behind and is as irretrievable now as that other paradise, the Garden of Eden.

There is another way, however. We spent some time earlier considering the basic datum of the Christian life: that by baptism we are incorporated by one Spirit into the one Body of Christ. If that is correct, then the question we are confronted with is not how we can build community, or how we can create a sense of community. The real question—one that has profound pastoral implications—is, how can we give appropriate expression in this place and at this time to the community we already are in Christ?

This distinction seems to me to be crucial. All sorts of organizations try to build community on the basis of friendship, common interests, shared tastes, and so forth. Whenever the Church tries to do the same, we get into trouble. The pastor decides to build a social club to foster community in the parish, but then has additional financial, staffing, and management problems, and still has to figure out a way of keeping up attendance in order to justify the investment. And the social club may or may not lead people into the church building. It is well meant but beside the point. The same is true of attempts to develop a community spirit in and through the liturgy: they invariably serve simply to obscure the real basis of our identification with each other— which is not ethnic, or socio-economic, or affective, or a matter of institutional pride or loyalty, but our common life in Christ.

More than half a century ago, Dietrich Bonhoeffer, in his book *Life Together*, offered a number of warnings against confusing Christian community with any other kind of community. Indeed, he argued, powerful experiences of community or strong attachment to the *idea* of community may well constitute grave threats to the Christian life:

> Just at this point Christian brotherhood is threatened most often at the very start by the greatest danger of all, the danger of being poisoned at its very root, the danger of confusing Christian brotherhood with some wishful idea of religious fellowship, of confounding the natural desire of the devout heart for community with the spiritual reality of Christian brotherhood. In Christian brotherhood everything depends upon its being clear right from the beginning, *first, that Christian brotherhood is not an ideal, but a divine reality. Second, that Christian brotherhood is a spiritual and not a psychic reality.*[8]

As if to emphasize the point, he goes on to warn:

> Every human wish dream that is injected into the Christian community is a hindrance to genuine community and must be banished if genuine community is to survive. He who loves his dream of a community more than the Christian community itself becomes a destroyer of the latter, even though his personal intentions may be ever so honest and earnest and sacrificial.[9]

It is important to protect the Church against unrealistic promises and expectations of community by recognizing that we are never going to have our longing for community satisfied in this life. Ultimately, our hunger for intimacy, for knowing and being known, is eschatological, and we shall only find the perfect balance between freedom and belonging, between public and private selves, in the life of the world to come.

In the meantime, it is important that we take seriously the realities of modern life. The realities include the following kinds of "facts:" (1) many of the people we are closest to, our "community" if you like, are scattered across the country and maybe even the globe; (2) we may or may not find a "home away from home" and a new collection of "significant others" in our local parish; if we make friends there that is a wonderful bonus; and (3) most of the people with whom we gather on Sundays will be people we do not know and whose faces we may not even recognize.

In light of these realities, surely not uncommon, we would probably be well advised to revise downward our expectations of what a parish can be and to reconcile ourselves to the fact that for the most part—except perhaps among those working full time for the parish or those closely involved in ongoing projects—many of our fellow parishioners are not going to feel close to us, nor we to them. We might as well abandon once and for all the ideal of intimate fellowship so often read into the Acts of the Apostles and the conception of the parish as an extended family, and become accustomed to the idea that the Church community is less a network of friends than it is, in Parker Palmer's striking phrase, "a company of strangers."[10]

This "company of strangers" will often have little in common beyond our common humanity and the Spirit poured into our hearts in baptism. This Body of Christ, in which there is neither Jew nor Greek, male nor female, slave nor free (Gal 3:28), cannot be true to itself if its unity is predicated on ethnic heritage, male bonding, socio-economic status, or the intimacy of first-name friendships. Indeed, the Body is most clearly visible for what it is when its members are most aware of their social divisions (male vs. female, rich vs. poor, black vs. white), and at the same time committed to not letting those divisions stand between them and not letting the solidarity within those divisions supplant the primary unity created by baptism. That is why clericalism is such an offense against the Church, and why the ghastly split between affluent, white suburban parishes and poor, black and Hispanic inner city parishes in the American church is a much more serious problem than many of the threats to the Christian life that seem to worry Rome and the bishops.[11] This then is the paradox: the parish is at its best, its most Catholic, when it is a real mix, a real company of strangers.

Too often we tend to regard the fact that we are strangers to one another in the parish as a sad fact, even to think of accepting the situation as it is seems like giving up. But is it giving up? Could we not take the relative anonymity of the average assembly as a starting point from which to explore how we might become a credible sign of the possibility of union with God and of the unity of human beings with one another? Could we not look for ways in which, precisely as strangers, we might be a sign of hope to the world? Parishes already consist of a small core of interactive people and a relatively large body of people who are "on the periphery," as it is said. Instead of regarding the people at the core as normative and their mutual involvement as a model for everyone else (which is neo-clericalism), what would happen if we accepted that it is the people on the fringe who are normative, that it is the stranger, not the friend, who is the typical "companion"?

The term "company," as Parker Palmer points out, suggests a number of people engaged in a common task. It also suggests a quality of hospitality shown to strangers in the performing of that task, as when we value their company. But etymologically, it comes from the Latin *cum* and *panis*: a company, made up of companions, is a group of people who break bread together.[12] Such an image, of course, has enormous resonance for Christians: not only the intimacy of the Last Supper, but the public event of the multiplication of loaves and fishes in which thousands of strangers were involved, sitting down on the grass in groups of hundreds and fifties (Mark 6:35-44). What would happen if we suggested that the thousands of anonymous people in the crowd were more the focus of Christ's intentions than the inner circle of named disciples? What difference would it make if we were seriously to consider that it is the people on the fringes of the parish who are normative rather than the core group of church regulars?

An example might illustrate the liturgical salience of the point. Most religious houses that celebrate the liturgy of the hours and Eucharist welcome visitors and may even encourage them to join the community's worship. The basic pattern nevertheless remains one in which individual "laypersons" attend the services of the religious community. At the monastery of Taizé in France, on the other hand, the relationship is reversed. What counts is the prayer of the Church that gathers from countries all over the world, the young people who come from north and south and east and west to Taizé to pray. They do not "join the monks." Rather, *they* celebrate the liturgy, and the monks provide a stable core community that gives a vision, a pattern, a discipline to the thousands of visitors, enabling them to pray. The core group serves the prayer of the crowd, instead of the crowd being welcomed and invited to join in the prayer of the group.

Let us push this a little further by exploring some of the possibilities opened up for the Church by the image of the company of strangers.

As a Community of Memory

We invariably speak of the parish as a "faith community" or "community of faith." This is certainly an admirable sobriquet for a local church, but it does tend to suggest that the members see themselves in exclusive terms, accentuating what they have in common that separates them from "outsiders." An interesting twist is given to the whole matter, however, if we interpret "community of faith" as the equivalent of what Robert Bellah calls the "community of memory."

In *Habits of the Heart* Bellah explores the profound individualism of Americans, traces its historical roots and evolution, and exemplifies all the different ways in which it manifests itself today. While demonstrating that individualism has a long history, Bellah warns that today as never before, it is coming to constitute a serious threat to this social fabric, and he calls for a renewal of communitarian consciousness and a new commitment to public values. In place of our current ideologies of pure undetermined choice—free of tradition, free of obligation, free of commitment—we need to recover, Bellah argues, a sense of community.[13] What he has in mind is what he calls "a community of memory that does not forget its past":

> In order not to forget that past, a community is involved in retelling its story, its constitutive narrative, and in so doing, it offers examples of the men and women who have embodied and exemplified the meaning of the community. . . .
>
> The stories that make up a tradition contain conceptions of character, of what a good person is like, of the virtues that define such character. But the stories are not all exemplary, not all about successes and achievements. A genuine community of memory will also tell painful stories of shared suffering that sometimes creates deeper identities than success. . . . And if the community is completely honest, it will remember stories not only of suffering received but suffering inflicted— dangerous memories, for they call the community to alter ancient evils. The communities of memory that tie us to the past also turn us to the future as communities of hope. They carry a context of meaning that can allow us to connect our aspirations for ourselves and those closest to us with the aspirations of a larger whole and see our own efforts as being, in part, contributions to a common good.[14]

Could a parish become such a community of memory and hope? Could a parish provide a place to tell stories with which people might identify? We have the biblical narratives of the Liturgy of the Word, but what of the stories of our saints and sinners? What of the stories of our church in America: both the church we have become and the churches across the ocean from which we come—the Irish, English, German, Polish, Italian and Spanish churches, the Roman Church and its papacy, the churches of the sixteenth century and the nineteenth, the stories of John Ireland and Junipero Serra, but also of the slavers and the *conquistadores*, and all the memories that make the discovery of America so ambivalent? Could our parishes become communities of memory and hope that would raise our sights and allow us to connect our aspirations for ourselves and our families to the aspirations of the larger society?

Such remembering is not just a parish exercise in consciousness raising, valuable as that would be. Liturgy is by definition an act of anamnesis, of remembering. At the Eucharist, we do what we do "in memory" of Christ, but all the sacraments, the liturgy of the hours, and the liturgical year are predicated on recalling the past and bringing it into the present in such a way that it might shape our future. That remembering is more than just the remembering of past events and people otherwise forgotten. First and foremost, it is a remembering of God who acts in and through human lives, in the present as in the past. And it is a remembering of God who acts for the salvation and wellbeing of the whole world. Liturgical anamnesis is an anamnesis of what God has done in particular times and places for people of all places and all times: "This is my body. . . . This is the cup of my blood . . . shed for you and for all, so that sins might be forgiven." Jesus did not die to save Roman Catholics alone or Christians alone. He is himself the representative of the whole human race, the firstborn of a new creation, the head of a new humanity.

It is essential, then, that the memory of Jesus not be kept alive merely as a private memory for individuals or even for the Church. Rather, we need, in Bellah's phrase, to "connect our aspirations for ourselves with the aspirations of a larger whole," and to recognize that the salvation we remember and celebrate is the salvation won for the whole human race, the redemption of the *whole* human story.

Karl Rahner speaks powerfully of this in an essay entitled "Secular Life and the Sacraments: The Mass and the World." After describing how God's grace permeates the whole of human existence and how it became visible in Jesus—"in a life made up of everyday things—of birth and toil, bravery and hope, failure and death"—Rahner argues that the liturgy of the Church is simply the place where we become most deeply aware of and committed to "this liturgy of the world":

> The world and its history is the terrible and sublime liturgy, breathing death and sacrifice, that God celebrates for himself and allows to be held throughout the free history of men, a history which he himself sustains through the sovereign disposition of his grace. Throughout the whole length and breadth of this colossal history of birth and death, a history on the one hand full of superficiality, folly, inadequacy and hate—and all these "crucify"—a history, on the other hand, composed of silent submission, responsibility unto death, mortality and joy, heights and sudden falls: throughout all this there takes place the *liturgy of the world*.[15]

The liturgy of Christ's death and resurrection is thus the culmination of the whole dramatic unfolding of living and dying, of warring and loving, of joy and sin and suffering and growth that makes up human history. In the Eucharist we celebrate that liturgy of the world and its redemptive culmination. The Church then cannot fail to be a community of memory without being untrue to its mission; it cannot properly remember the life, suffering, death, and exaltation of Jesus without at the same time remembering all the "colossal history" of which Christ's death is the culmination and which constitutes the "liturgy of the world." At the Church's liturgy we have the opportunity to identify with that whole unimaginable history of birth and death, of suffering and joy, which Christ took upon himself and redeemed when he became one of us. The Christmas collect, recalled at the preparation of the chalice, reminds us that Christ adopted our human condition to enable us to share in his divine condition. Is there any other way to share the divinity of Christ than by way of identification with all that makes up the human experience? Is there any other way to remember Christ except by remembering the world with which he identified?

Hence, to overcome the cultural momentum toward religious individualism, we would need forms of worship that actually cultivated such an awareness of the "liturgy of the world." Cultivating an awareness of the "liturgy of the world" is a rather different thing than political consciousness raising, though one outcome of serious liturgical participation ought to be enlightened engagement in the political processes of our own society and an interest in and concern for global issues. How can we move beyond the narcissism of "shared celebrations" to genuinely "public worship" without becoming sidetracked into "political liturgies" of whatever hue? It is not easy to predict exactly what such worship would look like, but my hunch is that since the main structures of our liturgy derive from an era in which liturgy was demonstrably *public* (as opposed to the more sectarian stage of the Church in the centuries of persecution), it may well be the case that these new forms would, paradoxically perhaps, be more "traditional." Maybe it would really be more a matter of finding a different style than of developing new forms. If so, what would a more public style of worship look like?

Liturgies celebrated by communities of memory as public worship would not be celebrated for the sake of togetherness, nor for private intentions. On the contrary, they would be marked by an awareness of the larger world as represented and spoken for in this assembly. They would be characterized by a certain gravity and fixity, presenting themselves as an objective undertaking into which we are invited to enter and to which we are invited to submit, rather than as a series of quasi-performances by presiders, readers, preachers, and musicians before a captive audience. Assemblies would not be whisked in and out in forty-five minutes. The proclamation of the scriptural word would be taken seriously, being heard and proclaimed as a word addressed to the assembly for the sake of the world, rather than to individual believers for their personal consolation. The prayers of the faithful would become a serious act of intervening with God on behalf of the peoples of the world and of all who suffer and are in need. The collection and presentation of gifts would not be confined to a ceremonial presentation of envelopes, hosts and wine, the one going no further than the business office, the others no further than the altar. Rather, the collection would be for the good of the poor, wherever they may be in the world, and only the minimum necessary would be skimmed off to maintain the liturgical and catechetical mission of the Church. Even the Eucharist itself would be a celebration of the generosity of God to *all* humanity of all places and times. In short, in prayer and in praise, in taking up the collection and breaking the bread, the community would never be able to think of itself except as a community of memory that knows no barriers of time and space.

Such an awareness would profoundly alter the frame of mind with which we would enter into a liturgical celebration. Today we tend to judge liturgies by what we get out of them and to think of participation as what we put into them. Rahner, in his vivid and inimitable way, describes a quite different frame of mind with which a person might approach the liturgy:

> He is profoundly aware of the drama into which his life is unceasingly drawn, the drama of the world, the divine Tragedy and the divine Comedy. He thinks of the dying, those facing their end glassy-eyed and with the death rattle in their throat, and he knows that this fate has already taken up lodging in his own being. He feels in himself the groaning of the creature and the world, their demand for a more hopeful future. He grasps something of the burden born by statesmen, their responsibility for decisions demanding all their courage and yet whose effects will be extending into an unknown future. He bears within himself something of the laughter of children in their unshadowed, future-laden joy: within him resounds also the weeping of the starving children, the agony of the sick, the bitterness caused by betrayed love. The dispassionate seri-

ousness of the scientist in his laboratory, the hard determination of those struggling to liberate mankind—all these find their echo in him.[16]

Rahner has more to say along these lines, all graphically portraying the frame of mind in which the Christian might properly approach the celebration of the liturgy. Just the adoption of such a perspective is often enough to transform one's experience of parish liturgy, so that liturgical renewal does not have to wait for the local pastor or liturgy committee to make obvious changes. On the other hand, the style of presiding, the demeanor of the ministers, the tenor of the verbal communications, and the choice of music perhaps need to yield to something a little more serious, a little more profound, a little less geared to popular taste, a little more conducive to sounding the mystery of our engagement with God and one another for the sake of the world.

But how can we develop a sense of our liturgies as *public* worship, celebrating in joy and in tears the whole colossal history of birth and death that is the "liturgy of the world"? We need to imagine ourselves as a priestly people.

As a Priestly People

Earlier we discussed the revolution in ecclesiology and in the understanding of the Church's mission represented by the move away from the Church as an "ark of salvation" toward a model of the Church as sacrament.

We also discussed the role of the Church and the liturgical assembly whom Christ associates with himself in the exercise of his priestly function before God on behalf of the whole human race. The assembly, as a realization of the mystery of communion, is an efficacious sign of union with God and of the unity of humankind, for it shares in the mediatorial work of Christ. In the liturgy we as a people represent all our fellow human beings before God, and invoke God's blessing upon the whole of humanity. Thus, the liturgy of the Church cannot be separated from its social mission—at least as long as its liturgy is truly the act of a priestly people and as long as its social mission is rooted in its sacramental nature, i.e., in the Church's own attachment to Christ through submission to the Spirit.

Whenever we celebrate the liturgy, therefore, it must not be for our own benefit so much as an exercise of our vocation to represent humanity before God. We must learn to pray the prayer of the liturgy with the voice of the whole Church. At the risk of appearing repetitive, it is important to look again at some elements of the liturgy from the point of view of praying them as public worship. Those prayers we already looked at for their inward dimension can now be looked at for their outward dimension.

The advantage of prescribed prayer, and especially of the psalms, is that it is precisely the alien quality that enables us to pray beyond ourselves, on behalf of the stranger half a world away or in the county jail, on behalf of those who at this moment lie dying, suffering violence, or even leaping for joy. In and through the words of the psalms we overhear the voice of the Christ, the Everyman, who identified with us all for the sake of all.

The psalms are not without their limitations, but what sometimes appears as their most serious limitation is actually a strength. Which of us on any given day can be sure of being able to identify on the basis of our own personal experience or as an expression of our own current mood with many of the sentiments expressed in the psalms? Can we expect a concordance of words and personal feelings? Does that make the praying of the psalms unauthentic? Not at all —as long as we allow the words of the psalm to guide our minds and hearts into a prayer that is alien, the prayer of Another, in whom all the joys and griefs of all the ages are taken up as his prayer to the one who is God of heaven and earth, God of all the ages.

One of the primary expressions of that high priestly prayer as it surfaces in our liturgy is, of course, the general intercessions offered at the conclusion of the liturgy of the word. These are the "prayers of the faithful," that is to say, of the baptized. In baptism we were anointed with chrism on the head and told: "[Christ] now anoints you with the chrism of salvation, so that, united with his people, you may remain for ever a member of Christ who is Priest, Prophet and King." But ancient as this ritual is, the prayers of the faithful and their association with baptism are even older. Back in the second century St. Justin wrote at Rome:

> After we have thus washed him that is persuaded and declares his assent, we lead him to those who are called brethren, where they are assembled, and make common prayer fervently for ourselves, for him that has been enlightened, and for all men everywhere, that, embracing the truth, we may be found in our lives good and obedient citizens, and also attain to everlasting salvation.[17]

Notice that Justin sees these prayers as an expression of civic responsibility as well as a "means of grace." The same sense of the responsibility of the baptized for the wider society of God's people is reflected in the *General Instruction on the Roman Missal*, n. 46, which suggests that the intentions for prayer should be ordered as follows:

(a) for the needs of the (whole) Church,
(b) for public authorities and the salvation of the world,
(c) for those oppressed by any need,
(d) for the local community.

Contrary to what is commonly done, the *General Instruction* neither prescribes petitions that summarize the main points of the homily, nor makes provision for private "personal intentions." If the directives are followed, the prayers of the faithful make us lift up our eyes, broaden our horizons, and make our own the concerns, griefs, joys, and anxieties of the whole human community.

Strange as it might seem, the same has to be said of the word of God. For just as the world addresses God through the Church at prayer, so God addresses the world through the listening Church. In short, like the incarnate Word himself, the word of God is given "for you and for all," being addressed not to us alone but to the world through us. Pope John XXIII once remarked that Christians were the eighth sacrament and the only sacrament the nonbeliever could receive. In much the same way, those who hear the word and take it to heart will become living embodiments of God's word. The word is given us to be passed on, but is it not passed on on billboards and TV witnessing so much as in the quality of the Christian life lived well. That is what Paul VI in his apostolic exhortation on evangelization called the primary form of evangelization: the Christian life that moves the unbeliever to ask what it is that enables people to live that way.[18] Thus even the most word-shy can become a powerful messenger of God's word. At least such would seem to be the point of the parable of the talents (Matt 25:14-30): the word we are privileged to hear at the Sunday assembly is given us to spend, i.e., to put into circulation in the larger world.

Even the Eucharistic Prayer, so much at the heart of the Church that it was for centuries kept secret from the unbaptized, stretches our horizons and fosters a more global awareness. It does not so much recall "Christian history," still less "Catholic history," as the whole history of the human race, from the creation and fall onward. It is not tribal history but global history, the history of humanity read as the history of God. And its vision of the future is equally inclusive, for it prays for the unity of the whole Church and of the whole world, and for the unity of the living with the dead in that one kingdom which is God's goal and end for the world. And the eucharistic elements are not merely natural products. Since they are not only God's gifts, but also "the work of human hands," they are inescapably part of the enormous, complex, and ceaselessly productive system that is the world's economy. The bread and wine placed on the altar are the fruit of *someone's* toil, the product of *someone's* labor, the means by which *someone* somewhere has struggled to earn a livelihood. Thus, even the central and most sublime and intimate of the Church's sacramental symbols is tied in with the world of work and economics.

CONCLUSION

A priestly people. We do not stand around the altar simply for our own benefit but because it is our vocation to stand before God on behalf of the world. Over and over again, the liturgy confronts us with reminders of that wider connection and resists our desire to privatize, to control, to narrow the ambit of God's grace. By the very nature of its being symbolic, the liturgy is also ambivalent. It is so easy, so natural to think of the liturgy of the word as a service of instruction or edification and nothing more, to make the assembly an occasion of belongingness, to shut out the world and indulge in cozy self-delusion.

> We thank you for counting us worthy
> to stand in your presence and serve you (Eucharistic Prayer II).

That could ring smug and self-satisfied: "I thank you, Lord, that I am not as the rest of humankind." But set against the whole background of the vocation of Israel and the Church, it is the prayer of a people assuming the responsibilities of their vocation. We thank you that you have counted us worthy

> to serve you on behalf of those who do not know you;
> to pray on behalf of those who do not know how to pray;
> to intercede for those who cannot plead for themselves;
> to hear the word for those whose ears are attuned elsewhere;
> to cry for mercy for those who do not know they need it;
> to offer sacrifice on behalf of those who do not know that death
>   and suffering have been redeemed;
> to celebrate communion for the lost and the lonely;

to serve you for those who do not know how to serve;
to thank you on behalf of those who do not know the name that
is blessed above all other names.

So our assemblies are big and anonymous, as are the cities we represent; but their inhabitants are redeemed and their loneliness, too. The liturgy of the Church is proof that strangers can be companions, recognizing the Stranger in the breaking of the bread.

Out of the sense of being a priestly people, a community of memory, a people who will not forget or escape into fantasy, arises a sense of solidarity with the rest of humanity, and especially with those who suffer, those who are powerless, and those who feel most keenly in their own flesh or their own spirit the terrible liturgy of the world.

The liturgy requires of us a setting aside of the quest for personal satisfaction; it demands self-abnegation, self-emptying, self-forgetfulness, so that our emptiness may be filled with the memory of Christ and with the fullness of his Spirit, in whom we know we are one with all God's people.

Outside the liturgy, participation in the work of Christ continues in the form of solidarity with the suffering. The paschal mystery we rehearse ritually cannot be detached from the paschal mystery lived by the victims of violence, poverty and disease, by those who are marginalized and oppressed, by the "little ones" of this world. The prayer that rises like incense is the prayer of the ovens of Dachau, the prayer of the streets of Calcutta, the prayer of the woman beaten by her lover, the prayer of the child tortured by his own parents, the prayer of the hungry of Mexico's barrios, the prayer of the AIDS victims. The litany is endless.

In the liturgy we join our prayers with theirs, put their prayers into words. A priestly people. A people who can offer in memory the sacrifice of the whole Christ, the passion of Jesus and the passion of the poor, the "little ones" of our generation.

". . . Pray, brothers and sisters, that our sacrifice may be acceptable to God the Father almighty. . . ."

Notes

1. "The Liturgy, The Basis of Social Regeneration," *Orate Fratres* 9 (1935) 541.

2. Ibid., 542 (emphasis added).

3. "The Scope of the Liturgical Movement," *Orate Fratres* 10 (1936) 485.

4. *The Christian in the World* (Collegeville: The Liturgical Press, 1939) 134 (emphasis added).

5. LG 16.

6. LG 1.

7. Robert Bellah, et al., *Habits of the Heart. Individualism and Commitment in American Life* (Berkeley: University of California Press, 1984) 134ff. and 71–75, respectively.

8. *Life Together*, trans. John W. Doberstein (New York: Harper & Row, 1954) 26 (emphasis original).

9. Ibid., 27.

10. See Parker J. Palmer, *Company of Strangers. Christians and the Renewal of America's Public Life* (New York: Crossroad/Herder & Herder, 1983).

11. "As society became divided along racial and economic lines [in the postwar economic boom], a two-tier church emerged. One level is white, middle-class and suburban; the other is brown and black, lower class, and urban. Neither one talks very much to the other and the lower class church feels especially alienated from the rest of the American Catholic Church. Bridging this gap and effectively responding to the needs of lower-class, black and brown Catholics is perhaps the greatest challenge church leaders face as American Catholicism enters the closing years of the twentieth century." Jay P. Dolan, "American Catholics in a Changing Society: Parish and Ministry, 1930 to the Present," ed. Jay P. Dolan, et al., *Transforming Parish Ministry. The Changing Roles of Catholic Clergy, Laity and Women Religious* (New York: Crossroad, 1989) 311.

12. Palmer, 10.

13. Bellah, 152–55.

14. Ibid., 153.

15. "Secular Life and the Sacraments: The Mass and the World," *The Tablet* 225 (March 13, 1971) 267 (emphasis original). See also Rahner's "Considerations on the Active Role of the Person in the Sacramental Event," *Theological Investigations* XII, trans. D. Bourk (New York: Seabury/Crossroad 1976) 161–84 (on the active participation of the layperson in the reception of the sacraments).

16. Ibid.

17. *I Apology*, c. 65 in E. C. Whitaker, *Documents of the Baptismal Liturgy* (London: SPCK, 1970) 2.

18. *Evangelii nuntiandi*: Evangelization in the Modern World (December 8, 1975) 21.

Afterword

It can be said that North Americans are living in an age of cultural transition, a kind of liminal state in which we are invited to discern how the contours of a modern culture coexisting with a postmodern culture are shaping our worldview, including our religious and spiritual perspectives. As evident in this book, Mark Searle understood the values of modern culture and concerned himself with the influence of these values on the capacity of Christians to participate in communal worship. In recent years, we can add to the mix of cultural values certain traits that appear to characterize the postmodern mindset, which are perhaps attempts to address the disappointments of the modern culture.

In particular, it seems that what has surfaced in this time of liminality is first, the desire for interrelationality, which pushes against a focus on the individual self. In other words, modern people are becoming more deeply aware of their basic need for right relationships and for a sense of belonging to something larger than themselves. Second, people are realizing that scientific reasoning simply cannot explain everything in life. Science and technology have no doubt brought about many achievements, but people have also witnessed science and technology gone awry, e.g., the destruction caused by nuclear weapons. Third, the modern myth of human progress is undermined by the stark reality of human sin and evil that is manifested in horrific acts, e.g., terrorist attacks, genocide in Rwanda, and the holocaust. Finally, people in this age are undoubtedly more globally aware than ever before. We need only watch television, surf the Internet, or use our cell phones to feel instantaneously connected to people of all continents.

The few contours of the modern–postmodern age that I have noted here are important to appreciating the significance of the insights and challenges Mark Searle holds out to us in *Called to Participate*. Mark

Searle appreciated the weight of modern cultural values and their potential effects on a Christian's desire and ability to engage in objective ritual behavior. I suggest that the pathway into the deep structures of liturgy Mark Searle articulates so clearly continues to be relevant in this era of transition.

It seems to me that we live in a time when there are opportunities to be seized, ones brought about by an emerging postmodern culture. As already mentioned, many long for interrelationality, for connectedness. Participation in the Church's liturgy, if understood as Mark Searle understood it, carries the potential of responding to this need of modern–postmodern people by rehearsing them in living in right relationships with God and others.

In addition, given the fact that not all of the world's problems can be solved by new technological inventions, that devastating events continue to happen in spite of, or even because of, scientific advancements, and that deplorable crimes against humanity continue to be committed, perhaps people are more willing to turn to religion and accompanying worship practices in order to make sense of life. Once again, Mark Searle's invitation to give one's self over to the Church's liturgy—surrendering in trust to the ritual itself, participating in the faith and prayer of Christ, and like Christ, offering one's self to God—provides an avenue for contemporary people to immerse themselves into ultimate meaning.

Lastly, there is an opportunity in our increasing social awareness and appreciation of diversity of peoples in the Church and in the world. As Mark Searle points out, Christians have a responsibility to turn towards the world and to participate in the work of bringing about a more just, a more compassionate society. The Church's liturgy, according to Mark Searle, shapes attitudes intended to help us carry out this responsibility.

Mark Searle had a remarkable ability to appropriate to present times what is core to Christian worship, and at the same time, he impels us into the future. The legacy he leaves to us is not to be underestimated, for it is nothing less than an exhortation to plumb the depth dimensions of the Church's liturgy for the sake of ourselves and for the sake of the world.

Anne Koester

Index